PieceByPiece

Key pieces for effective ministry to children today

Tammy Preston

Copyright © Tammy Tolman (née Preston), 2008. Discoverylearningseries.com

First published 2008
This edition published 2022 by Intergenfaithresources.com

All rights reserved. No part of this publication may be reproduced, stored in a retrieval system, or transmitted, in any form or by any means, electronic, mechanical, photocopying, recording or otherwise, without the prior permission in writing from the publisher.

ISBN 978-1-921161-14-8

All scripture quotations, unless otherwise indicated, are taken from the
HOLY BIBLE, NEW INTERNATIONAL VERSION® NIV®
Copyright ©1973, 1978, 1984 by International Bible Society.
Used by permission of Zondervan. All rights reserved.

Cover design by Peter Shirley
Page layout and design by David Gray – www.mooloolabaweb.com

Sam and Georgia Tolman. Sam is the Sports Stacking National Australian Record Holder.

This book is dedicated to Sam and Georgia Tolman, my children. They give me the greatest pleasures and greatest challenges in life. They motivate me to endeavor to be on the cutting edge of children's ministry, in order that they might truly come to know Jesus in a real and lasting way.

Foreword

It's wonderful when all the pieces in life make sense.

I must be one of the most fortunate people alive. I grew up in a home with a Mum and Dad who loved each other, they loved us, and they loved Jesus.

Life mostly made sense for me as a child and that was largely because the adults in my life knew what they were doing. They lived with purpose, they lived with consistency and they lived with a great under girding story about God and his love.

I grew up going to Sunday school. That's a long time ago, but I still remember with gratitude a man called Paul Goesling. He was a Fireman who taught my Sunday school class. He loved his wife, he loved Jesus, he loved us - and he told us the best stories, some from the Bible and some from his life. He reinforced a picture of life that has held me safe to this day. I'm grateful.

Children need help. There are so many homes where the pieces just don't fit. So many children are growing up in situations where adults don't know what they are doing and they have "nibbled their way to lostness".

How important is ministry to children? It's the difference between life and death. In this book Tammy Tolman has created a road map to effective ministry to children. The impact of a caring adult who knows how to make the pieces fit can be the difference between a life of trust in God and a life of wandering disappointment and despair.

May God move your heart to want to make the pieces fit for the children of your community.

Piece by piece we can do it. Good on you, Tammy. Well done.

Dr. Allan Meyer
Senior Minister
Careforce Church

Contents

INTRODUCTION 1

CHAPTER 1: ARE YOU PUZZLED?
OUR CHILDREN ARE JUST AS PUZZLED AS WE ARE ABOUT LIFE 3

CHAPTER 2: THE PRESENT PICTURE
THE STATE OF CHILDREN'S MINISTRY TODAY 21

CHAPTER 3: THE GUIDE PICTURE
WHAT IS GOD'S PLAN FOR CHILDREN?..................................... 31

CHAPTER 4: THE CORNER PIECE
JESUS MUST BE OUR CORNERSTONE
YOUR RELATIONSHIP WITH GOD IS A VITAL PIECE OF THE WHOLE PLAN 57

CHAPTER 5: THE VITAL EDGES – 1. LEADERSHIP
YOU CANNOT BUILD A STRONG MINISTRY FRAMEWORK
WITHOUT POSITIVE LEADERSHIP 71

CHAPTER 6: THE VITAL EDGES – 2. COMMUNITY NEEDS
UNDERSTANDING THE COMMUNITY WE LIVE IN IS VITAL
TO BEING EFFECTIVE IN MINISTRY 83

CHAPTER 7: THE VITAL EDGES – 3. TEAM BUILDING
MINISTRY WILL BE AS STRONG OR AS WEAK
AS THE TEAM WE WORK WITHIN 97

CHAPTER 8: THE VITAL EDGES – 4. DISCIPLESHIP
THE PURPOSE OF THE MINISTRY IS TO INTRODUCE CHILDREN TO JESUS;
THEREFORE, WE NEED A DELIBERATE PROCESS OF GROWTH FOR OUR KIDS .. 111

CHAPTER 9: THE CONNECTING PIECES
– CONNECTING PIECES, LIKE THE ICING ON A CAKE,
ENSURE THE PICTURE SHINES THROUGH CLEARLY TIM & RACHEL HUGHES... 135

CHAPTER 10: THE CONNECTING PIECES – 1. ACTIVATING
– TO ACTIVATE SOMEONE IS TO GET THEM TO ACTIVELY
TAKE A PART IN THE LEARNING PROCESS................................... 141

CHAPTER 11: THE CONNECTING PIECES – 2. EXPERIENTIAL
– OUR KIDS NEED TO LIVE EXPERIENCE, NOT JUST CONSUME IT............. 151

CHAPTER 12: THE CONNECTING PIECES – 3. 'EDUTAINING'
– WE NEED TO BOTH EDUCATE AND ENTERTAIN
TO COMMUNICATE EFFECTIVELY... 169

CHAPTER 13: THE CONNECTING PIECES – 4. RELATIONSHIP
– OUR ABILITY TO BUILD RELATIONSHIPS IS THE KEY
TO CONNECTING TO PEOPLE TODAY 181

CHAPTER 14: WHAT KEEPS A PUZZLE TOGETHER?
– LOVE, COMMUNICATION, UNDERSTANDING OUR DIFFERENCES AND
ENCOURAGEMENT CAN BE CONSIDERED THE 'GLUE' OF MINISTRY – ELEMENTS
OF DESIGN THAT KEEP THE PUZZLE FITTING PERFECTLY TOGETHER......... 195

CHAPTER 15: CAN THE PICTURE CHANGE?
– NEEDS AND MINISTRY ARE ALWAYS CHANGING;
SOME THINGS NEVER CHANGE 213

WHAT PEOPLE ARE SAYING ...

There is an interesting conversation in Lewis Carroll's *Alice in Wonderland,* between the Cheshire Cat and Alice. Alice asks, "Would you tell me, please, which way I ought to go from here?" To which the cat responds, "That depends a good deal on where you want to get to." It is the story of children's ministry throughout our world today. Children's workers often know they need to move on from outdated, ineffective programmes, but have no idea where to move on to! Children's workers who are so focused on doing, that they rarely have time to look up and ask the big questions.

- Why am I doing what I do?
- Is there a better way?
- Do I really make a difference in these children's lives?

If you are one of those children's workers then STOP! Find some space. And read this book!

Tammy Tolman not only addresses the 'why', but also presents the 'how'. She shows us, not only where we are going, but also how we get there. This book will help you understand 21st century children, but more importantly, how to reach them. You have in your hands a significant key to winning this generation for Jesus.

Mark Griffiths, Author and Lecturer, London, UK
Author of "Don't Tell Cute Stories – Change lives!"

"Our children face a changing and complex world. There is no greater task for the church today than to effectively love, serve and equip our children. Tammy passionately and excellently outlines a picture of 21st century children's ministry with vulnerability and honesty. I valued being stretched and challenged by many of Tammy's stories. This is a must read for pastors, children's leaders and parents."

Simon Hood
Logosdor Ltd

Tammy has certainly put her heart and soul into the content of this book in order to inspire and instruct those involved in ministries where children are involved. Her passion to see transformation take place in lives is the theme that weaves this book together – not only the transformation of those being ministered to – but also of those doing the ministering.

Jo Hood
International Director, mainly music

This is an incredibly good book! The way in which Tammy faces the true position of where we are at today with regard to children and where the church is at is absolutely frightening! I love the way she not only shows the stark reality of where we are at, but so amazingly comes up with such simple and straightforward solutions. Not only does she present these in the text itself, but also in the questions and challenges given at the end of each chapter.

Her willingness to pinpoint prevailing attitudes that need to be overcome by adults, especially amongst Christian leaders as well as Christian parents is very courageous! Her approach is very straightforward and refreshing, while at the same time being really creative.

Gary Parsons
Founder – Kids of Gold Camps
Victoria Australia

INTRODUCTION

Introduction

When my son was 4-years old, I watched him try to do a puzzle. He was putting pieces every which way in odd spaces. Of course, they didn't fit, and as I felt his frustration, the teacher in me stepped in and began guiding him about how to put a puzzle together. Thankfully, he is a compliant child and was open to my leading. As I verbalized the process to him, I saw the sheer joy and satisfaction on his face when he was able to complete the puzzle and see the picture in its finished form.

There are many similarities between ministry and doing a puzzle. I see so many people struggle in ministry, placing people and programs in a free spot and hoping that it all comes together. Yet with a simple process, ministry can be so much more effective.

Sam and I began by sorting out the pieces. We looked at each piece and saw that there are three kinds of puzzle pieces. There are the edges, the corners and the middle pieces. Then by looking at the guide picture we began by placing the corner pieces, then putting together the edge pieces and then finally the middle pieces. With the guide picture always as a point of reference, while putting together the puzzle was always a challenge, it was a positive experience for my son.

As we piece together the vital aspects we need to effectively minister to our children in the 21st century, it is my prayer that you, too, will find it a challenging but positive experience as you serve God and the children in your care more effectively.

I encourage you to take the time after each chapter to work through the Questions and action steps that are set out for you in order for this book to help you to be more effective in your ministry today.

CHAPTER 1

Are you puzzled?
Our children are just as puzzled as we are about life

After speaking at a conference dealing with 'Children in Worship', a member of the audience came to me in tears. She said she had been working with kids for fifteen years and had never considered they could actually worship God. My first thought was, "Well, what have you been doing with them all this time?" This woman explained that all the examples I had just given them regarding what *not* to do – making children sit down, be still, and sing songs that just get the wriggles out – was what she thought it was all about! I am continually amazed at what leaders in children's ministry think their purpose is.

A farmer told this story about how cows end up on the road lost:

> *A cow is nibbling on a tuft of grass in the middle of a field, moving from one tuft to the next, and before you know it he ends up at grass next to the fence. Noticing a nice clump of green on the other side of the fence, the cow stumbles through an old tear in the fence and finds himself outside on the road. "Cows don't intend to get lost," the farmer explained, "they just nibble their way to lostness!"*

The farmer didn't know it, but he was talking about more than cows. None of us intends to wander from the green pasture of God's Voice![1]

---

[1] Michael Yaconelli, *Dangerous Wonder: The Adventure of Childlike Faith*, NavPress Publishing Group, 1999, pp. 14-15

So many leaders and teachers are puzzled. We 'nibble our way to lostness' doing the same old things we have always done and find ourselves puzzled by today's child. We are puzzled because the kids won't listen to us anymore. We are puzzled because kids just aren't interested in the Ten Commandments, much less knowing what the Old Testament is. We are puzzled because kids only seem to answer questions with a shrug and an "I dunno". We are puzzled because kids would rather stay home and play their PlayStation than go to a church program. Children's leaders are puzzled because when faced with a problem, kids would rather turn to the Internet for answers than ask anyone who might actually know. Mostly, we are puzzled because we feel lost in the world that our kids live in daily. The truth is, we are not just in a changing world, we are in a whole new world.

I remember the Christmas my parents gave me a DVD player. Now let me put this into context. I love movies; they are my escape from reality. I love to put movies on and watch them at home since there is rarely anything on TV worth watching. Needless to say, I had a wonderful and considerable collection of videos that I had been buying for a number of years. I had become quite proud of my collection and had accumulated nearly all of my favorite movies.

I ought to have seen it as an incredibly thoughtful and generous gift when my parents gave my husband David and I a DVD player, especially since at the time they were quite expensive and certainly not something we were able to buy. Yet as we opened it, what do you think was going on inside my head? "But I don't need a DVD player! I am happy with my video player and I have all my favorite videos… You mean I have to start recollecting? That's crazy, especially now that videos are getting cheaper! (They were being superseded by DVDs…)"

David was excited about it and declared it an awesome present, as he firmly believed at the time that the quality of DVDs was so much better than video. Meanwhile, I was trying to hide my disappointment. I didn't want to transition into a whole new world; I was comfortable with the old one.

CHAPTER 1 - ARE YOU PUZZLED?

You see, our kids are in a whole new world. It is not simply a matter of changing – of improving what we already have. It requires a complete transition of thoughts and processes. Even as I write this, I am aware that before long DVD players, too, will be on the way out as they introduce the next best way to watch movies. For many church leaders, there will need to be a radical change of methods and style if we are going to really connect with the kids of today.

One of my favorite authors, Leonard Sweet, would say that we are like aliens in this whole new world. As a parent, I am amazed at how consuming it is to keep up with the language and information that our kids are being immersed in. It is not just a matter of *talking about change* any more; we need to *be in transition.* Just as I had to be prepared to transition to a DVD player and leave my videos behind, we must be willing to transition to the new world if we are going to prevent ourselves from becoming aliens who can no longer communicate to our kids.

> *...we are like aliens in this whole new world*

Today, our kids live in the world of virtual reality, surfing the net, yogurt sites, SMS, emoticons, advergaming, cybersquatting, and YouTube. If these are all foreign words to you, you need to spend a brief amount of time on the Internet with a 10-year-old and let them open up a whole new world for you.

We live in an information age with which we can't keep up. One out of six teens told the Barna Research Group in 1998 that they expect to use the Internet as a substitute for their church-based religious experience.[2]

Futurists say that 95% of the jobs today's high school students will hold in their lifetime have not even been invented yet. Here are some of the job titles of the future, according to Danish futurist Rolf Jensen:

---

[2] Leonard Sweet, *SoulTsumani: Sink or Swim in New Millennium Culture,* Zondervan, Grand Rapids, 1999, p. 420

- Director of Mind and Mood
- Chief Imagination Officer
- Creatologist
- Intangible Asset Appraiser
- Director of Intellectual Capital
- Visualiser
- Assistant Storyteller
- Chief Enactor
- Court Jester[3]

As a children's worker it is important to me that I stay 'at the cutting edge' of what is going on. I am continually amazed at the journey this has taken me on. I can be feeling young in my mind when in an instant my son unintentionally makes me feel like an alien.

I went on an excursion with my son as a parent helper. We were going to an historic house that was set up to show the children what it was like to live in the past. I showed Sam and two other boys around and helped them answer their worksheets. We came to a big box, and as I opened the lid I realized it was a record player. I began to explain to the boys what it did and how it worked and said that I'd had one when I was little. Sam looked at me, his eyes round with amazement, and said, "Wow, Mum! You're from the olden days!" The boys looked at each other and giggled, and right then and there I felt so old! It doesn't take much to realize that the reason we might feel so puzzled is that we are in a *whole new world.*

When was the last time you stepped into the world of a 10-year-old boy or girl? When was the last time you read the latest magazine for kids this age? When was the last time you watched a music video show? If the answer is longer than 6 months, then no wonder you are puzzled!

---

[3] Leonard Sweet, *SoulSalsa: 17 Surprising Steps for Godly Living in the 21st Century*, Zondervan, Grand Rapids, 2000, p. 50

CHAPTER 1 - ARE YOU PUZZLED?

Do you know what this is? If so, what does it say?

"*Wilufon mewnugt hom?*"

No, it is not a dialect from the *Yu-Gi-Oh!* world. (That would be much more complex!) This is called 'kidspeak'. It is the SMS for, "Will you phone me when you get home?". The SMS language is a form of shorthand for the mobile phone that kids use all the time.

I am not suggesting that we even keep up with the intricate worlds our kids live in, but at least staying in touch with the everyday things would be helpful. It is simply a matter of connecting with kids regularly. We need to listen to them, watch them, read and take note of the community around us and the things that influence us all. More importantly it is our responsibility to question and seek answers for why these things are happening. The worst thing we can do is to accept it all and simply go along with it because it is 'in', or to just stay the same and never change the way we do anything.

Mike Yaconelli says: "The critical issue today is dullness. We have lost our astonishment. The Good News is no longer good news, it is okay news."[4]

> **Mike Yaconelli: "The Good News is no longer good news, it is okay news.**

Our kids see church and Sunday school and think '*dull*'. Not only have they lost their astonishment; I believe we teachers have as well. We are puzzled because the latest curriculum, which we are pinning all our hopes on, is not at all interesting to the kids; and we don't know what to do about it. The influx of curricula and resources is wonderful in so many respects, but not when we feel we do not have the right to question and change or reject stuff that does not relate to our kids. We continue to use the same material and methods because it has worked for twenty years, and yet our children leave bored and conclude that Jesus is *dull*. This leaves us puzzled.

---

[4] Michael Yaconelli, *Dangerous Wonder: The Adventure of Childlike Faith,* NavPress Publishing Group, 1999, p. 24

Of course Sunday school seems dull compared to the world that Middleton and Walsh describe as "...a cable culture. We can simply switch channels to sample other, easily available worlds."[5] We cannot compete with this world, and we are not meant to. If anything, we are to be picking up the pieces of the mess that this world leaves behind. It is not real, is not healing, it does not contain the answers this generation is seeking.

Not only are we puzzled, but so are our children. The postmodern world view that says that everything is 'right' and you can do what you want is very frightening for our kids. They are thrown into this world view and it strangles them. As we work through this together, you will discover that there are many issues for this generation that are not very positive. This makes it imperative that we stop being puzzled and begin to offer some answers, wisdom and guidance for this generation. Children will look for answers to their many questions anywhere that someone will speak to them. It's time that God had a stronger voice in this generation through His people.

Let's flesh out a few of these big issues. If we do not understand the picture, we'll never know what to connect with to reach these kids. Let's look at some of the things that puzzle our kids.

OBSESSED WITH THE WAY THEY LOOK

The media and marketing have become the major influence in this area for our kids. The reality is, the only way your children are not going to be influenced by media and marketing in western society is to keep them trapped in a box all their life. Of course this is neither possible nor legal, so we must find better ways to help our kids through it. The fact is, as a Christian parent this is one of the most challenging things I do. At a very young age our children are getting messages from everywhere.

It is important to constantly be counteracting the culture that says you have to wear a certain thing, eat certain things, and do certain things to be 'cool' or acceptable. When I was growing up, the first time

---

[5] J Richard Middleton and Brian J Walsh, *Truth is Stranger Than It Used to Be: Biblical Faith in a Postmodern Age*, InterVarsity Press, Downers Grove, 1995, p. 42

I ever used a hairdryer was in high school. Now 4-year-old boys are using them. When children walk into your ministry, what is the first thing you say? "Hi... You look great today. Hey, cool shoes!" You are trying to be encouraging, but what are you saying in that comment? Sometimes we need to make sure that we are not feeding the lies of 'consumerism'.

When I was just starting in ministry, I went to the USA for a holiday, and it was the time when LA Gear clothing was beginning to be the rage in Australia. When I got to the US, LA Gear shoes were really cheap. Purple is my favorite colour, and there was a great pair of purple LA Gears for just $19.95 US. I love getting a bargain so I bought them. I will never forget the moment when I got home and went to church on my first week back. Instead of the kids looking me in the eye and saying, "Hey, it's great to have you back. How was your trip?", they looked straight at my feet and said "Hey, LA Gears! They're unreal... they are so cool!" It felt like I spent the next few months explaining to the kids that I got them really cheap in America, because it was so important to me that they didn't think that I would spend $100.00+ on shoes (which is what they were priced at, at the time).

Now, some of you will be saying, "What's the problem?" To a degree we are all sucked into fashion and having the latest thing. I really struggle with this and believe that as Christian parents/leaders there must be somewhere where we deal with the fact that materialism, consumerism and the obsession with how we look are out of control in our society.

FAMILY BREAKDOWN
I know it seems that, as a society we have been talking about this for so long, but I don't believe we have seen the worst of it yet. I am not just talking about families that actually break down physically. There are many forms of breakdown. I believe that a really big issue for the present is to help parents be parents. They are crying out for guidance, help and support.

Over the years I have run a number of community programs for kids that help them with 'Life Skills'.[6] When we ran an 8-week course that offered teaching and guidance on issues such as setting boundaries, managing anger, conflict resolution and making friends, families from all sections of the community were virtually busting down the doors to get their kids into the program. We were unashamed about the program teaching Christian values and they didn't care, as long as we helped them. When they dropped their kids off for the afternoon, many of the parents chose to hang around. They started talking to the other parents and soon enough we had a little self-help group going on in the foyer. As a result, we started supplying tea and coffee, food, and a counsellor who could help guide a discussion for the parents. That proved to be a great link for these families into the church.

> **We cannot minister to children in isolation, because the family is integral to the child's ability to change his or her circumstances.**

This highlights a very important point. We cannot minister to children in isolation, because the family is integral to the child's ability to change his or her circumstances. We need to be resourcing and supporting parents as they raise their children.

When you look at their families, some kids just don't seem to have a chance these days. As I was writing this book, I had a scary experience. I was at a pool with my kids. They were playing with some other children in the pool. I saw a young boy about 5, and an older sister, about 7, jump into the pool near my kids. Their father walked up to his kids and said to the older sister "Watch Jordan, you know he can't swim. I'm going to the bar for a drink." I was thinking "You have got to be joking!" So of course I couldn't stop watching his kids.

---

6 "High Five" - www.life4kids.com.au
 "Kids With Courage" - www.careforcelifekeys.org/aus/

Sure enough, five minutes later, I looked to see this little boy going under the water and beginning to drown. I jumped up and yelled to my son, "Sam, the little boy beside you is drowning, grab him and bring him here!" As he did that, the older daughter panicked and jumped onto her brother, causing them both to begin to drown. Sam was now trying to carry them both to me as I waded through the water to grab them. The girl was going under screaming, "Save me!". A number of others watched as I pulled them out of the water and checked to see that they were okay, but there was no sign of their parents.

Once Jordan had recovered, I asked him where his parents were. In response, he ran straight to his mum who was in the spa talking on her cell phone. I walked over to inform her that her son had nearly drowned. She stopped talking on the phone to hear the story, and then proceeded to relate the story to the person on the other end as if it were some kind of funny joke. I left with my heart beating and feeling rather angry at the mother's response. She continued to talk on the phone and it wasn't long before her little boy was back in the water and being saved for the second time by an elderly man. I couldn't believe what I was seeing and couldn't help but think that some kids just don't have a chance of growing up feeling valued and secure.

The family is in great need of support, care, training and prayer. We need to view the picture of children's ministry with the care and support of families being an extremely important piece.

QUESTIONING SEXUALITY

In 2004, I was in America speaking at a conference. The big issue in the media was whether it was right to allow gay people to marry. There were talkback shows and news coverage on every channel. At that time there were four states that allowed gay marriage, and gay people were flocking there by the thousands to get married. I watched a talk show host interview three people, one of whom was a Christian minister. When asked, "Do you agree with gay marriages?" he answered, "I don't believe it is a lifestyle that God agrees with, so I don't either." The host's response was simple.

"Well, that's fine if you don't agree with it. But what right do you have to tell anybody else how to live?"

The confusion continues today, and the lines have become more and more blurred. The result of the postmodern worldview is that 'truth is relative to the individual'. We live in a "conspiracy of ambiguity" in which no one is prepared to say or define anything. This leaves kids confused. The world encourages them to question their sexuality and everything seems acceptable. The Bible says 'there is only one truth, and that is God's truth', but there is still ambiguity in how that truth is understood across Christendom. We must be willing to walk lovingly with children and families and hear what God says about sexuality, otherwise the world's voice will be the loudest.

OPEN TO SPIRITUAL THINGS

This is a subtle but powerful and scary issue for our kids today. Yes, our kids are very spiritual. In fact this whole generation is very spiritual. Unfortunately that has nothing to do with Jesus and Christianity.

Here is an example. I believe the Harry Potter series had a strong influence, changing the rules about what is spiritually acceptable in society. In the first movie, Harry Potter and the Philosopher's Stone, Voldemort says to Harry, "There is no good and evil. There is only power and those too weak to seek it".[7] This principle changes everything. Many Christians encourage their children to read these books. I have had many a conversation with parents and children's workers over these phenomena, many Christians believe that Harry Potter is harmless. After I read the first two books and watched the first movie, I had seen enough to know that my children did not need to see them. We talked about the fact that Harry does not get his power from God. He gets it from the Evil One. Even though he may do good things with it, that doesn't mean he is on the side of God.

This is just the beginning of a generation where the line has been crossed. There is a lot further to go and we will see where these phenomena – a spiritual awakening started by the Harry Potter series – will take our society in the next ten years.

---

[7] JK Rowling, *Harry Potter and the Philosopher's Stone*, Warner Brothers, 2001.

CHAPTER 1 - ARE YOU PUZZLED?

The following quote captures what I believe is the current spiritual trend being followed by our kids: "Whereas just a decade ago younger people were saying no to church but yes to Jesus, increasing numbers are now in search of a transcendent spirituality in which Jesus no longer occupies a central place."[8]

Oprah Winfrey talks of 'spiritual things' but they are not Christian. She is one of the most powerful and influential people in television in America and does some amazing things for people. However, there's a subtle undertone to her message that does not necessarily lead people to God, but rather to self or the higher being of your choice. She uses a language that is very spiritual, but like much that is deemed spiritual in this generation, it is still based on self and relative truth.

> *Whereas just a decade ago younger people were saying no to church but yes to Jesus, increasing numbers are now in search of a transcendent spirituality in which Jesus no longer occupies a central place - Eddie Gibbs & Ian Coffey*

Even Barbie is into it. Mattel has finally taken Barbie into the spiritual world of witchcraft with its Secret Spell Line. There are three dolls that come with an assortment of spell books, magic powders and an assortment of potions. *Children's Ministry Magazine* made this comment about it: "One of the most telling responses from the world of witchcraft was posted at triplemoon.com by someone named Crow Wing. "Have we become this mainstream?" There is actually a Barbie doll that only practices 'white magic'? I guess it's a product of all the teen witch shows. Now I've heard it all".[9]

I was reading our local paper recently and there was a four-page spread all about the 'Mind, Body and Soul'. It had articles addressing

---
[8] Eddie Gibbs & Ian Coffey, *Church Next: Quantum Changes in Christian Ministry,* 2001, p. 11

[9] *Children's Ministry Magazine,* Jan/Feb 2004, p. 15

questions such as "Is the Bible relevant?", then surrounding this article were ads for 'The Reiki Relaxation Centre', 'Psychic Connections', 'Spectrum Healing', Yoga and an article that talked about how Eastern Art satisfies the body and the spirit.[10] These were all lumped in together and presented as acceptable choices. That's where the deception lies.

THE NEED FOR STABILITY

In a world that is constantly changing, our kids need a place where something is stable. The family was traditionally this place and still can be for many, but increasingly, even the family is a place where things can be very unstable. For many of our kids, consistency is a real issue.

When I was growing up, my family all had an evening meal together. Dinner time was a family time, and it was something consistent and stable that I just took for granted. I am amazed at how many families very rarely have a meal sitting all together. There is reassurance in traditions and things that become regular experiences for a family. They can be simple and seem insignificant at the time, but they are actually very important to a child's sense of security.

Now when my own family sits down together for a meal each night, we have created a tradition called 'Best Part Of Our Day'. As we finish saying grace, the kids nominate who is going to be last to talk about the best part of their day. Over the meal time, we all take turns to listen to each other share. It has become a great time for stopping and listening to each other, important for the kids in learning to reflect on their day, and also fantastic to hear what everyone has been doing. It is such an important part of the meal for our children that even when visitors come over or if we are at a restaurant, they still demand that we share the best parts of our day, and everyone around the table must be involved.

Our little ritual has proven a great a way to hear what is important to our children. Each of us feels encouraged, as it turns out that often the best part of our days is being together and having a meal after a

[10] *Illawarra Mercury,* March 17, 2004, pp. 38-39

long day at school and work. It has been a great chance to say to the kids that being together now is what is important to us all.

What ways do you bring stability to your children? I am fortunate that my childhood memories are full of experiences that promoted stability for me. I am convinced they are a strength upon which I live my life today. Experiences like always eating together at the table at night , holidays, Dad taking all my friends to youth group – all piled up in the car (probably illegal now), - special shopping outings with Mum, and many others.

> **What ways do you bring stability to your children?**

We would spend the weekends at Physical Culture competitions, and knowing that my Mum was there, waiting all day for me to do my routine, was very special to me. My parents were, and still are, always people I could count on. They were always there supporting me whenever I did something - always that stabilizing force. It sent me out into the world with confidence.

In Luke 3:22b, God says to Jesus, "You are my son, whom I love; with you I am well pleased." We all need a sense of security and sense of significance. Even Jesus did. There is so much evidence to prove that it is a basic human need. When our children don't get it, it makes it harder for them to succeed in life. I am very aware that as children's workers we can add to the stability of their world, or be another place where children experience constant change. In a world that is crying out for stability, we are not helping the problem when we work on roster systems and see a constant turnover in ministry roles in our children's programs.

There is a reason why teachers in the school system have a class for one year. It takes that long to establish relationship and stability in a classroom in order to be able to do something significant with the children. When they go to church or children's ministry they are lucky to see the same person three weeks in a row, and then we wonder why they don't feel like Sunday ministry is a stabilizing force for them. We need to reassess how and why we structure our ministries if we really want to make a lasting impact on a child's life. We will look further at practical ways to connect with kids in later chapters.

SENSE OF HOPELESSNESS FOR THE FUTURE

In one of Oprah's magazines, an article captured my attention. It was entitled 'Ten Good Reasons to Have Faith in the Future.'[11] I was shocked as I read through it. The article began: "Today's world is a terrifying place. Every day we wake up facing the frightening realities of our age: terrorism, weapons of mass destruction, pollution, domestic violence, psychotic criminals who steal children right from their own beds". It then continued to say that a simple act of hopeful thinking can get you out of the fear zone and can replace anxiety with happy anticipation. The article proceeded to outline the ten reasons we can feel good about the future.

The first was feminism: "The fact that the weaker sex is growing stronger just may save the world." Second on the list was Starbucks. The article used the New Testament to back this up: "I love the New Testament image of Jesus napping on a boat during a storm. Peaceful revolutionaries change the world by great efforts and small comforts: one hot bath, one morning walk, one quiet act of self-care at a time. Today, a mocha malt frappuccino is my favorite splurge, what's yours?" The third reason to feel good was "the freedom to live in sin". I couldn't believe what I was reading! It stated: "That people can clash at the level of basic values but tolerate one another's differences gives me enormous hope for the future".

I won't give you the next seven. It just got worse. If this is what we have to look forward to, no wonder we are so messed up as a generation. Our children need more hope than this and a sense of what's to come. We need to give them a purpose for living now and a sense that our future is to live forever with God.

Just recently, we received the news that my husband's uncle had died. He was old and in pain, so in many ways it was a good thing. But

---

[11] *O, The Oprah Magazine*, March 2004, pp. 79-81

CHAPTER 1 - ARE YOU PUZZLED?

the sad reality is that he died from alcoholism and didn't know Jesus at the time of his death.

When we told the children that Grandma was sad because her brother had died, my son's response was, "I am sorry that Grandma is sad, but isn't it a good thing, because now he is with Jesus in heaven." My husband and I smiled at each other. We didn't tell him that he may not be there, it is not our place to judge, but we were happy that he saw death as a pathway to be closer to God. We hope that we can continue to foster that with our children. It is a hope that no other form of spirituality can promise.

Can I also add that when this sense of hopelessness is coupled with the current openness to spirituality it can become dangerous. In the movie *The Never Ending Story*, the character known as 'The Nothing' says, "People who have no hope are easy to control. Whoever has control has the power".[12] We are living in a time when a witch can talk openly about being a witch in the boardroom of companies on Channel Nine's *Today Show*[13] and everyone feels this is totally acceptable conversation for a morning chat show. She (the witch) and a business man were talking about casting spells on people and how he uses this to advance himself in the workplace.

> **People who have no hope are easy to control. Whoever has control has the power**

There is power in 'spiritual' things being seen as acceptable. These days even the ABC is something I feel my children cannot watch without major screening because of the continual theme of witchcraft and sorcery in the shows they play between 3.00pm and 6.00pm. This is a power that is not accidental, because for children who have no hope, the thought of power to fly and to cast spells is very attractive. When this concept is presented as simply fantasy, they are captured.

---

12 *The Never Ending Story,* Warner Bros. Entertainment, 1984
13 Channel 9, Friday, 22 July, 2005

This is something that needs to be a major focus for Christian parents and leaders today.

So, what do we do with a puzzling future, knowing that our children are: obsessed with how they look, want to be entertained, have everything materially, struggle to find role models to learn from, are always negative and stressed out, feel alienated and alone, have very little family experience, need to feel they belong, have been told all their life that truth is what they make it, question sexuality, and are looking for the ultimate experience? In the midst all this, I believe the postmodern generation want to know God – not know *about* God or about religion – but to *know* God and experience God as a person.

> **Isaiah 55 "All you who are thirsty, come to the waters**

Isaiah 55: 1 proclaims: "All you who are thirsty, come to the waters". Our children are thirsty, and because they are thirsty they will taste anything! They are looking for leadership. I love the line in the movie *The American President* when Lewis (the character played by Michael J Fox) is talking to the president about leadership. He says, "People want leadership, Mr. President, and in the absence of genuine leadership they'll listen to anyone who steps up to the microphone. They want leadership. They're so thirsty for it they'll crawl through the desert toward a mirage and when they discover there is no water, they'll drink sand". The president replies, "People don't drink the sand because they are thirsty; they drink the sand because they don't know the difference!"[14]

This is what is happening to our kids. They are looking for direction; they will listen to anyone who chooses to speak to them. It is time to stop being puzzled and start to have some answers for our kids.

We have only begun to touch on the big issues for this generation. The puzzle is complex, but it is our job to make sure the picture is clear for us as leaders of these children. Our children are puzzled because children's ministries very seldom address these issues. As

---
[14] *The American President,* Universal Pictures, 1995

leaders we are puzzled because we seem unaware that to address these issues is the *purpose* of children's ministry.

ACTION STEP

- Go and rent a movie that all the kids are watching today. Work out why they are watching it! What do you think God would have to say to this movie?

  _____
  _____
  _____

- Buy a kids magazine, or surf the net and see what kids are reading and seeing on the Internet.

  _____
  _____
  _____

- Watch TV during the kid's time slot and study what they are watching. (You will probably be shocked)

  _____
  _____
  _____
  _____
  _____

PIECE BY PIECE – TAMMY PRESTON

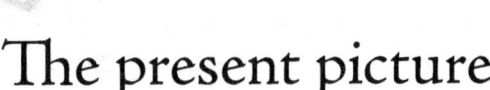

The present picture
The state of children's ministry today

There are ministries scattered across every country that are doing some amazing things with the children in their community. However, much of the church and outreach ministries are crumbling and struggling to survive. While children's workers are united and renowned for working well together, the majority of our children today are lost. The impact of the good work that is being done remains minimal.

For a long time there was no clear picture of the value of children's ministry.

Ten years ago, when traveling by plane to speak at various conferences, businessmen would snigger when they found out what I did for a living. "I am a children's pastor," I'd explain, and they would reply, "What do you do? I've never heard of such a thing!"

Ten years ago, while working as a children's pastor (which meant working fulltime and being paid two days a week), a senior pastor approach me and offered me the job of youth pastor. He was offering me a fulltime job, and felt he was doing me a favour because I would be paid a fulltime wage. I was crushed to hear his suggestion, and answered, "With respect, I'm called to work with children; I'm not called to work with youth. Thank you, but no thanks". His reply stunned me. He said, "Come on Tammy, grow up – there will never be a job for a fulltime children's minister. Take the youth job and you can do children on the side. I'll give you time to re-think my offer."

Although the attitude towards the value of children's ministry is changing, it still has a long way to go. The picture of children's ministry is yet to be seen as something of equal value to many of the other ministries in the church.

George Barna's book *Transforming Children into Spiritual Champions* has begun to bring balance to this picture. George Barna clearly outlines the sad fact that we are losing a whole generation because we currently have the wrong picture. I believe we are in an exciting age where we will see some amazing things happen with this generation. However, this will only happen if we can learn to connect with the children and empower them, as the next generation of leaders, to live differently.

Referring to the USA, George Barna makes a staggering statement which confirms something I have felt for years. He says, "Church leaders often view the children's ministry as a 'Loss Leader'– a retail term used to describe the marketing of a product that loses money but generates a sufficient payback through ancillary benefits. Children's ministries are frequently marketed to adults because research shows that millions of parents want their children to have a positive church experience...Viewed from that angle, many churches support ministry to children because kids are seen as the 'bait' that enables the church to land the real treasure – i.e. adults – rather than as a valuable, if unrefined, treasure in themselves."[15]

If we are really going to look seriously at effective ministry to children in the 21st century, we have to look at the practical ways that we can break down this mindset in our church leaders. Unless the perceptions of those in the position to make significant changes in structures, staffing, allocation of finances, and preaching and teaching are altered, we are just looking at ways to improve a maintenance ministry. Ultimately that will not be effective.

---

[15] George Barna, *Transforming Children into Spiritual Champions,* Regal Books, Ventura, 2003. pp. 40-41

CHAPTER 2 - THE PRESENT PICTURE

You might be thinking, "That is a bit extreme!" Yet just one simple example George Barna cites underlines the imbalance in our current value systems. The USA spends "roughly 68 times more money per capita on caring for the average felon than on a church's ministry to a spiritually hungry child."[16]

When it comes to communication, we have followed a school-based process in our churches for a long time. Yet children are walking out of church at the age of 13 with a worldview that is not Christian. The greatest things we can bring to kids in our communication are the life skills with which to make good decisions in their everyday lives. Most children are leaving Sunday school after 13 years believing that Jesus Christ has nothing to say to them about their everyday decisions. I am seeing children aged 9-10 years actually deciding that Jesus has nothing to teach them that is relevant to their daily life.

> *George Barna: The USA spends "roughly 68 times more money per capita on caring for the average felon than on a church's ministry to a spiritually hungry child"*

George Barna discovered that of all the children he surveyed, more than half believed that there are no absolutes for morals and ethics, that when Jesus Christ lived on earth he committed sins, and that the Bible does not condemn homosexuality. 75% believed that the devil does not exist – he is just a symbol of evil, that a good person can earn their way to heaven by doing good things, that we are born morally neutral and make a choice to become good or bad, and that spiritual and moral truth can only be discovered through logic, human reason and personal experience.[17] Clearly, if this is what we are communicating to our children, we need to look seriously at what we

---

[16] George Barna, *Transforming Children into Spiritual Champions,* Regal Books, Ventura, 2003. p. 41

[17] George Barna, *Transforming Children into Spiritual Champions,* Regal Books, Ventura, 2003. p. 41

are doing. We need to not simply change the children's program, but transition to a whole new way of ministering to children.

> Most American Christians are too familiar with Christianity. After all, this is a 'Christian nation'. A large percentage of Americans still attend church on a fairly regular basis. We know about God and Jesus and the Bible. We've heard the stories, sung the songs, gone to Sunday school, been baptised and confirmed. We know all about God. God is part of our culture, part of our upbringing, part of our daily lives. I recently realized just how dangerous it can be to become comfortable with what's familiar... Ironically, our 'Christian' nation has become oblivious to a terror that can liberate us. We have become comfortable with the radical truth of the gospel; we have become familiar with Jesus; we have become satisfied with the Church. The quick and sharp Bible has become slow and dull; the world-changing Church has become changed by the world; and the life-threatening Jesus has become an interesting enhancement to modern life."[18]

Without a doubt, I am confronted by the same issues as I travel around churches in Australia.

Dr. Mary Manz Simon,[19] an author and corporate consultant on trends affecting the children's Christian marketplace, gives some facts about children in America today that she believes we need to be aware of. It gives us a little insight into the present picture:

- This is the generation that claims that Homer Simpson is the greatest person in the world.
- 60% of sixth grade children are going home alone.
- 20% of children's new friends are made over the Internet.
- Escapism is something that they are all craving; 2003 had more blockbusters than ever before.

---

[18] Michael Yaconelli, *Dangerous Wonder: The Adventure of Childlike Faith*, NavPress Publishing Group, 1999, p. 113

[19] Dr. Mary Manz Simon, Speaker at "Children's Pastors Conference", San Diego, 2004

CHAPTER 2 - THE PRESENT PICTURE

- There is a fear that children need to get back to the basics. She says even the most influential TV shows are trying to help children get back to the basics. Recently, Nickelodeon had a campaign that ran for a number of months called "Let's just play". It was aimed at encouraging kids to play with each other.
- Family is very quickly becoming the big need in the USA. 80% of kids are still saying that their parents are the most important person in their life, and the family motto here is "It's we – not me – that are family" and "Family is where no one gets left behind".
- 50% of today's kids live through divorce.
- 2.4 million grandparents are now raising their grandchildren.

It is interesting that even with regard to the Christian message, Hollywood is making a bigger impact upon this generation than the church is.

In February 2004, Mel Gibson released *The Passion Of The Christ*. Although there were mixed feelings about it, the movie took the USA by storm. The Church appeared to jump on board with this film and supported Mel Gibson all the way. Mel Gibson was certainly good at marketing. The film was R-rated and very violent and graphic, yet it opened in more theatres in the USA than any other movie in years.

I was in the US at the time and was fascinated by the way the media responded to the 'Jesus' in the movie. I watched a talkback show late one night *(Real Time with Bill Maher)*. He had a panel of people responding to the movie. One of the guests was the actor who plays 'Gandalf' in *Lord of the Rings*. He said he felt that while the depiction was probably realistic for those days, he couldn't understand what the 'big deal' was with this guy. There were hundreds of crucifixions. Why was his death anything special? The host replied that he had to agree. His problem with the movie was that it claimed that this man, Jesus, could save our sins, when we all know that we can save ourselves – we don't need anyone to do that for us. As the studio audience applauded, I sat amazed at this worldview. This presenter really believed that he could save himself. It is a very real belief across the western world, and it is frightening how important it is for people to believe that they can do what they want and no one can tell them otherwise.

> **Dr Ruth Powell: The current generation of school-aged children is likely to be the first where the majority has had no experience of church**

In Australia, Dr Ruth Powell of NCLS Research says "The current generation of school-aged children is likely to be the first where the majority has had no experience of church....This means that the majority of current school-aged children may have few or no religious reference points from their upbringing".[20] We do not have a culture of going to church. To get kids and families to hear about Jesus we must be on the cutting edge and have something that connects with the kids or they will not come. Overall, it means that the kids we reach, we really impact; but we are missing too many.

So, in a world where the picture is crumbling and Jesus takes very little priority in many children's lives, how are we going to change this picture?

> **children are people who need Jesus**

We must begin with realizing that children are people who need Jesus. They are not 'bait' to capture 'real' people. I believe this issue comes from a deep-rooted belief that our children are to be seen and not heard; that they are to be taught until they become adults, when ministry to them can then be taken seriously. So often, we have taken the approach that children are like wet sponges – that you just stuff in as much as the sponge can fit, and hope that when it is needed it spills out and is useful to them. The statistics show that this process of ministry is not working. It is time to seriously change the present picture.

---

[20] Dr. Ruth Powell, NCLS, MEDIA RELEASE - 7th November 2003 *National Church Life Survey*, 2003

CHAPTER 2 - THE PRESENT PICTURE

Confirmed by ACS (Australian Community Survey) data, many churches will have noticed that the number of children attending church services or Sunday school is not as great as it was in the past.[21] With this transition that has occurred over the past 40 years, we as adults have forgotten that our children live in a world that is very different now. For many years, children have been taught to question and not just take all that they are given at face value. Children have been encouraged to investigate and probe for more, and not to be satisfied with just what they are given. Their life experience has taught them that the people who are supposed to care for them and protect them may not do that, and they must learn to survive at a very young age by themselves.

The media throws so many options at children that they are overwhelmed, and yet they are addicted to the next best thing in the hope that it satisfies the deep need for purpose and love that they have inside. This postmodern world has told them that truth is what you want it to be and that they are the masters of their destiny. Children are out there trying to be the masters of their own world, and we sit them down for one hour a week on a Sunday morning and try to tell them a two-dimensional, sweet story about a man called Jesus, and think that it is going communicate to this generation's needs.

Don't misunderstand me. Of course Jesus can meet this generation's needs, but as the communicators of this message we must take some responsibility for the way in which this is done. We have to know what the present picture is in our community before we can do anything about changing it. We need to discover ways to actually turn these frightening statistics around. It will take more than change; it will take a major transition.

---

21 Dr. Ruth Powell, NCLS, MEDIA RELEASE - 7th November 2003

 **ACTION STEP AND CHALLENGES**
Discover your present picture!

1. Have a look at the statistics of your current community and even what they are predicting for the future. You should be able to find this at your local government departments.

   _____
   _____
   _____
   _____
   _____

2. What would be the top 3 needs in your current community today?
   1. _____
   2. _____
   3. _____

3. What are you doing about them?
   1. _____
   2. _____
   3. _____

4. Spend some time asking the parents of the kids you minister to what they feel would be most helpful in way of support to their family?

   _____
   _____
   _____
   _____
   _____
   _____
   _____

5. Take your team to another Church and see what they are doing that is really working.

_____
_____
_____
_____
_____
_____
_____
_____

6. Connect with the local community – festivals, community events etc. Serve them and discover the needs of the people of your community as you serve.

_____
_____
_____
_____
_____
_____
_____
_____

PIECE BY PIECE – TAMMY PRESTON

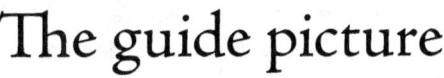

The guide picture
What is God's plan for children?

As people filed into the room, I gave them all a piece of a puzzle. It was a large floor puzzle, so each piece was the size of a person's hand. I had set up a large table and asked everyone, once they were settled, to gather around the table and see if they could put the puzzle together. I had taken out many of the edges and the corners and left the people with all the middle pieces and no picture for reference. Then I watched for their response.

Some people got right in there and tried to talk to others and work out how to solve this problem. Some just threw their pieces on the table for the others to sort out, while the rest sat quietly holding onto their piece and watched the chaos. After about ten minutes, the table had a few pieces connected in the middle of the table but mostly was a scattered mess. It was obvious that they were not close to finishing. I asked how people were feeling during this exercise and the overwhelming response was frustration!

It's a very similar story when we minister to children. We bring our piece to the table, but we are not sure what do to with it, where it fits in, or what the point is. Mostly, without a guide picture as a reference, the puzzle is always much harder to achieve. It's not impossible, depending on how long you have to do the puzzle, but it can be a frustrating process without the big picture in sight.

Without a reference point, it's likely the puzzle will never get finished before people will give up. The trouble with the 'children's ministry puzzle' is that we are talking about people's lives and that's not something we can play around with just for the challenge or, alternatively, simply give up on when it gets frustrating.

Before my frustrated group had completely given up in despair, I asked each person to take their pieces back and do it again, but this time with a guide picture. This time it was finished within 6 to 7 minutes, even with the bits that were missing. Having the big picture made all the difference. The guide picture gave everybody a point of reference for where they were heading as a group and where their individual part might fit in.

THE BIG PICTURE

It may seem an obvious point, but we all need a vision – that is, a guide picture. We all need to know why we are doing this ministry, what we are aiming to achieve, and how we are going to do it. I know it's something that is talked about in business, even in the church as a whole, but rarely do I see a written statement and guide picture for the ministry we are involved in with children. Unless we begin to address this issue, we won't actually change the problems that ministry to children is facing today. When I use the term 'ministry to children', I want to broaden the idea that we are just talking about a 'Sunday School Program' in a church. If we are going to understand the big picture that God has in mind for children in this generation, we must open our eyes to the diverse ways that God will use people to minister to children today.

When I was writing this book and thinking of what I believed should be the 'big picture', my first thought was of kids smiling and happy faces. But I soon realized that this image was not really reflective of what the big picture ought to be. We all want to see kids smiling, but if that is all we see then we are no different to Time Zone or a Wiggles concert. We must be about more than simply seeing kids happy, no matter how many we are talking about.

CHAPTER 3 - THE GUIDE PICTURE

I realized that in reality, the BIG picture is all about *children* reaching and growing toward Jesus. While this isn't a simple picture, and there will be many ways to see it achieved, it's still the big picture we are aiming to see completed. The great commission (Matthew 28) calls us to "go out into all the earth and make disciples of all nations, baptizing them in the name of the Father, the Son and the Holy Spirit". Unless we see kids discipled, we are missing the whole point of what we are doing. They must be discipled in Christ – not in you, or the program you run. (Especially when they are young, to them there isn't much difference between you and God to begin with). Unless they are connected with God and have found a real relationship for themselves then we are only drawing a crowd. So, what does this mean for you and your ministry?

We must begin with our theology of children's ministry.

It's very important to work through these issues for yourself. It will shape the way you do ministry. The easiest way to see what people really believe is to watch the way they respond to the things that they see. Let me work through a number of incidents in my ministry experience that demonstrate our theology relating to children and what we can often believe. These examples have come from a range of ministry experiences. You can be sure that wherever Christians gather there will always be misconceptions of what children can handle and how we must handle them.

> *You can be sure that wherever Christians gather there will always be misconceptions of what children can handle and how we must handle them*

"I DIDN'T THINK YOU'D GO THAT FAR!"

If you believe children can be saved and need the Lord, then the Gospel message and discipleship will be a big focus in your ministry.

I remember one Sunday morning when I presented the Gospel message to the children and about 30 gave their heart to the Lord. It was a wonderful morning and I had just finished praying with them down the front. By that time, parents had begun coming in to pick up their children and some were sitting at the back of the room.

As I walked up towards the door, I had a parent come and say to me, "Gee, I didn't think you would go that far!" I was a little taken aback by the comment and wasn't quite sure what he meant. I asked him to explain. He said that he was surprised that I had actually asked the children if they wanted to receive Christ and then prayed with them. He wasn't angry, but I think that he was surprised that kids could accept Christ. It obviously wasn't in his theology that children could do that.

This incident made me realize a few things. One is that many parents are happy for their kids to come to children's ministry programs, especially when the kids themselves want to come, but they do not necessarily have the desire for their kids to actually have a deep relationship with Christ. The frightening thing is that parents have handed over their responsibility to spiritually raise their kids to children's workers at school and church, when it should be the other way around. As children's workers, we should be supporting and helping the parents do their job. If this is part of your big picture, then what you do and where you spend your energies as a children's worker should reflect this.

This issue needs to be addressed with Christians in general, not simply left as a big issue only for those who work with kids. You will need to work out how you are going to handle issues with your kids' parents. For example, if the father had been angry and this had happened, how would you have handled that? We must never minister to kids in isolation from their parents. If they don't believe their kids can be saved then you will be working in direct conflict with the way they are bringing up their kids.

Remember that we are here to aid the family. This may be challenging, particularly if they are preventing their children from coming to Jesus. If this is the case, you must be committed to working with parents to help them understand how Jesus sees their kids. If they still do not believe children can come to God you are going to have to respect that and continue to pray for them and their kids.

> *One day children were brought to Jesus in the hope that he would lay hands on them and pray over them. The disciples shooed them off. But Jesus intervened: "Let the children alone; don't prevent them from coming to me. God's kingdom is made up of people like these. Matthew 19:13-14*[22]

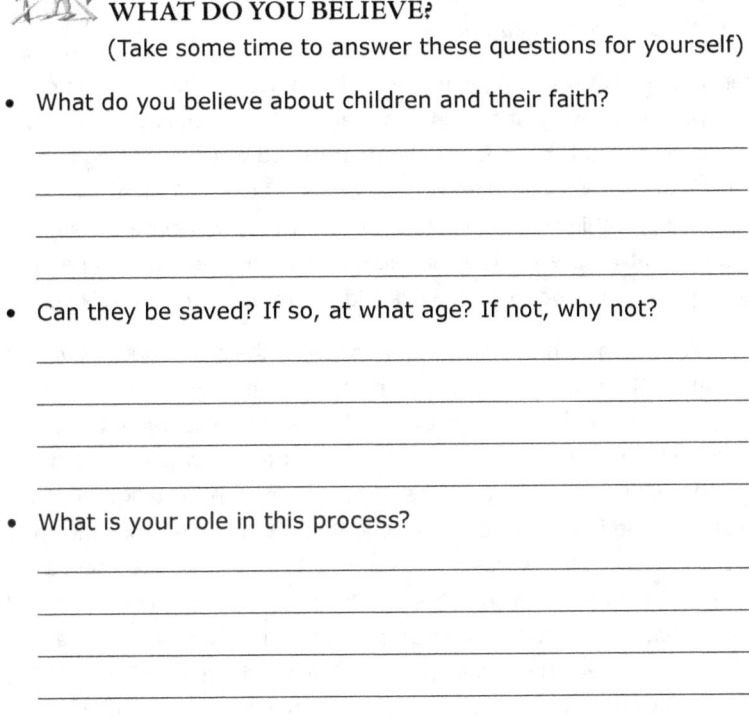

WHAT DO YOU BELIEVE?
(Take some time to answer these questions for yourself)

- What do you believe about children and their faith?
  _____
  _____
  _____

- Can they be saved? If so, at what age? If not, why not?
  _____
  _____
  _____

- What is your role in this process?
  _____
  _____
  _____

---

[22] Eugene H Peterson, *The Message: The Bible in Contemporary Language,* NavPress Publishing Group, 2002, page 1782

- Where do parents fit into the picture?

"I DON'T BELIEVE GOD SPEAKS TO KIDS!"

I remember at a camp a number of years ago we had finished a great ministry time at the end of the night, during which many kids were prayed for and touched by God. We had been singing a song that had become a favorite for the kids called *"Be Like You"*.[23] Do you ever find that God uses a song for a season to really move kids? Well this song was that song for this camp.

Later that night, I was lying in my bed when I heard a knock at the door. When you get a knock at the door late at night, you think the worst. So I sprang to my feet and opened the door to two worried looking female leaders. Now I was even more concerned, and I asked, "What's wrong?" They replied, "I think you had better come with us, we have a situation in our cabin that we are not too sure about." So I grabbed my jumper, put it on quickly, and proceeded to walk with them as they were talking.

They informed me that while they were all in their own beds having a time where they read their Bibles and prayed, one of the girls started crying. One of the leaders went down to her and asked her what was wrong? She replied by saying that she was praying to God to help her know that He was real, just as I had spoken about in my talk that night, and she felt God gave her a verse to look up. When she looked it up, it was the verse that the words in the song *Be Like You* had been based on. This non-Christian girl couldn't believe these words were in the Bible and that God had led her to them. She was crying uncontrollably. So I asked the leaders, "What's the problem? This is wonderful news!" They looked at me with worried looks and said, "But can this happen? I mean, she is just a kid!" After I finished praying with the child, I had a long talk to the

---

[23] "Be Like you" – Written by Tammy Tolman, Be Like you CD, 2004

leaders about God and how He can do what He wants and that age is no barrier. I am often shocked at the theology that people who work with children have about what God can and can't do with His children.

> If anyone causes one if these little ones to sin, it would be better for him to have a large millstone hung around his neck and to be drowned in the depths of the sea. Matthew 18: 6

 **WHAT DO YOU BELIEVE?**

(Take some time to answer these questions for yourself)

1. Do you believe that God wants to talk to kids?
   _____

2. Do you encourage the kids to listen to God?
   _____
   _____
   _____

3. If they wanted to share a word from God during your ministry time, how would you respond?
   _____
   _____
   _____

"NO, WE DON'T BELIEVE HE IS OLD ENOUGH FOR THAT"

I remember attending a ministry team meeting. The whole church team was gathered, and as we all presented our highlights for the week, I shared that 30 kids gave their heart to the Lord on Sunday. Instead of singing and celebrating (which I know the angels above were doing), there was a general murmur, and we moved onto the next person. I sat there and thought, "It's my responsibility to be an advocate for these children. I won't just babysit them for four years". My theology and guide picture forces me to act upon what I believe we are doing this ministry for.

The issue of baptism presented a bigger problem. I had run a two week course on baptism and a number of kids wanted to be baptised. As I worked through baptism with these kids, it was clear that it was important to them to take the next step. On taking this to the church ministry team, I was immediately asked their age, and told that they had to be 11 years old before they would be allowed to think about it. I remembered when the disciples turned the children away and Jesus rebuked them. I wondered what Jesus would do in this situation.

Our Children's Camp wasn't long after all this had happened. I remember after one night of worship, teaching and ministry, a boy in my church, who was about 11 years old, came to the front. He was a 'hard one' – one of those back seat boys who sit with their arms crossed and always look as if they don't want to be there. He was never naughty, just always in the background. He came to me with tears in his eyes that night and said, "Tammy, I believe God wants me to be baptised." I embraced him and we cried together and I prayed with him. It was such a wonderful moment.

As part of the Church of Christ, we are not allowed to baptise children until the age of 11. This means that any child that makes a commitment has to wait until they are 11 to be taken seriously. I thought, "Great, he is old enough, there won't be an issue with his baptism". But when I got home and told his parents, they said very politely, "Oh, no. We don't believe he is old enough for that. Sorry, we won't allow it."

There was nothing I could do because I had to respect the wishes of the boy's parents. I wept on the inside, as I feared this would be such a backward step for this boy. I do hold onto the truth that what God has started he will continue, but I personally do not want to be responsible for stopping a child coming to Jesus. I will still stand up and speak out for children and teach them the ways of God, knowing that it will take a while to challenge existing theologies.

Later that year we did baptise three kids in our service (him included) and many people raved about how precious it was. It began to open up a new wave of understanding for the kids and their families in the church.

CHAPTER 3 - THE GUIDE PICTURE

You need to know what you believe and be willing to teach it, knowing that you will come across many obstacles as you challenge the way we currently allow kids to experience God.

> Go out and train everyone you meet, far and near, in this way of life, marking them by baptism in the threefold name: Father, Son, and Holy Spirit. Matthew 28:19[24]

WHAT DO YOU BELIEVE?

1. Can children be baptised? If so, at what age? If not, why not?

_____
_____
_____
_____

"I DON'T THINK OUR CHILDREN CAN HANDLE THAT!"

In an endeavour to help kids go deeper, we started a discipleship group called *Friendzy* on a Thursday afternoon. It was a two-hour program that included games, eating together and hanging out together as friends, but in the middle of it there was a 40-minute small group time where the kids were actively discipled.

(It may take time for the leadership of our churches to understand the importance of this type of program, but in four years time when the kids graduate with a sound knowledge and active experience of Jesus in their life, they might come to see the value. Even if they don't, it's the picture God has given to me as a children's pastor, and I have to be faithful to that in whatever situation I am ministering.)

As a result, the children were learning about being a disciple of Christ. We had to begin another two ministries as a direct result of this discipleship focus. We created a KIA (Kids in Action) group, for those

---

[24] Eugene H Peterson, *The Message: The Bible in Contemporary Language,* NavPress Publishing Group,??

aged between 11 and 12 years old who were actively serving. Then when they became old enough for Youth Group, they became Junior Leaders. We were training a generation to serve God, to put what we have learnt into action, and to see God do amazing things when we give Him the little we have to offer.

As a part of the children's discipleship program, I wanted to take the Junior Leaders on a mission trip to Fiji. The parents and children were very excited and were challenged to raise their own money. Being the 'gung-ho' person that I can be, I was getting on with organizing the trip when I was called to the office of my pastor. He asked me what was happening. I shared the idea and how exciting this would be for the children's spiritual development. His response was, "I don't think our children can handle that. It's too dangerous and they are too young to have that kind of experience". This says a lot about a theology that doesn't believe children are meant to actually serve and reach out to people in other countries. They are obviously supposed to just learn about it in the Sunday school classroom.

I see changes of attitude slowly happening throughout the Church, but it won't happen by fighting these misconceptions verbally or being negative. Instead, we need to change the culture of the place. Don't give up! Hang in there for the sake of the children.

> **I am starting to see that you really believe that children can minister and serve God**

That same year we introduced Family Services. This was where we did intergenerational worship with the whole family. It was a carefully planned service with a team of people that were very interactive, and it involved people of all ages, but especially the kids. The congregation came to value these services as a highlight of the year and enjoyed doing something that was more interactive. They especially enjoyed seeing children using their gifts and beginning to serve God in powerful ways. I had a parent come up to me and say, "I am starting to see that you really believe that children can minister and serve God. It's really different to how I was brought up in the church. Keep up the good work; you're doing a great job".

> *Therefore go out and make disciples of all nations, baptizing them in the name of the Father, and of the Son, and of the Holy Spirit. Matthew 28:19-20*

 **WHAT DO YOU BELIEVE?**
(Take some time to answer these questions for yourself)

1. Can children serve? If so, will you let them teach or serve in the church service?

   _____
   _____
   _____
   _____

2. Are you serious about empowering kids to DO mission work or simply to TALK about it?

   _____
   _____
   _____
   _____

WHAT DO WE WANT TO ACHIEVE AS TEACHERS AND LEADERS?

George Barna conducted research on how pastors and parents felt about what was going on for their children each Sunday. Most felt happy with what their children were receiving, yet this conflicts with what the children are saying or understanding about God.

"74% of the pastors interviewed claim their church is doing an excellent or good job of getting kids to adopt a biblical worldview. In spite of that, we know that fewer than 5% of church kids who are born again have a biblical worldview by the age of 13".[25]

George Barna has some shocking figures about the lack of reality in the American churches' belief regarding what their kids are receiving at church. They seemed more concerned that they behaved themselves in class than with their spiritual journey. I see the same issues with Australian children as well. The question remains, "What are we valuing and what is important to us?" If we are serious about our children's spiritual wellbeing, we will be discovering ways to connect with what is really going on with our kids and finding ways to address these issues.

In his book *"Spiritual Parenting"* Charles Spurgeon had an insight about children that was beyond his time. It's a small but profound book. Spurgeon was England's best-known preacher and he is still one of the most quoted and published preachers who ever lived. He talks of children being "little lambs" and says that God commands us to "feed His lambs". He simply believes that they should be "taught" and valued as people who need to be discipled just as any adult does.

> **If there be any doctrine too difficult for a child, it's rather the fault of the teacher's conception of it than of the child's power to receive it, provided that child be really converted to God**

"If there be any doctrine too difficult for a child, it's rather the fault of the teacher's conception of it than of the child's power to receive it, provided that child be really converted to God".[26]

This speaks to many people today who believe that children cannot be saved, much less understand the truths of God. It's certainly a challenging statement. When we look at complex doctrines like the

---

[25] George Barna, *Transforming Children into Spiritual Champions,* Regal Books, Ventura, 2003. p. 124

[26] CH Spurgeon, *Spiritual Parenting,* Whitaker House, New Kensington, 1995, p. 8

CHAPTER 3 - THE GUIDE PICTURE

trinity, it reminds me of Paul when he says, "I have become all things to all men so that by all possible means I might save some" (1 Corinthians 9:22NIV).

As a trained educator, I have come to appreciate educators such as Erikson, Piaget and Kohlberg. Their teaching principles have helped me understand children better, so I can then communicate truth in a way that the children might understand. In his above quote, Spurgeon is addressing the fact that children can understand biblical principles; he isn't addressing how they best learn them. So while there may be an order of the things that children can learn, as Christian educators we must be able to answer the questions that the children will ask in a way that they understand.

I remember an 8 year old child in *Kid's Klub* a number of years ago asked me, "How could Jesus be God and yet die on the cross, with God watching Him?" This was a child wrestling through the issues of the trinity. In moments like these, we need to be able to help them understand. I must take responsibility for my failure if I can't help these children. It's not good enough to answer them with, "It's too hard for you to understand."

The more I work with children, in relationship and in an atmosphere that empowers them to question and take seriously the truths of Christ, the more I find these challenging questions coming from their mouths. We must be prepared with an answer, but first we must believe that with God's help they can understand difficult things and actually want to grow in Christ. "For nothing is impossible with God." (Luke 1:37 NIV).

Regarding ministering to children, Ron Buckland writes:

> *We must not expect too little from the child, delaying response until he reaches an age of accountability. Nor will we demand too much of the child, treating him simply as a little adult. We will pray for a work of the Spirit in lives of both evangelist and child....we will be calmly urgent about our task: urgent, for we know that apart from the*

Holy Spirit, the child will give increasing evidence of his sinfulness; calm, because we depend on the Holy Spirit as the ultimate agent of change.[27]

There are many abstract concepts that we need to be able to help make concrete for our kids. Couldn't this be said for everyone as they grow in their faith?

In experiments with children in Christian education settings, Doug Scholl of Harvard University found that there is an upward yearning in the child's mind for more mature modes of moral thought. Using the basic research fabric of Lawrence Kohlberg, Scholl contrived learning experiences using what he called a 'plus-one-match'. In this strategy, the level of moral thinking predominating in the group was noted, and then a child with advanced ways of thinking, usually one level above the majority, was used as the model to which other children's thoughts were elevated.[28]

We won't find this in educational theories, as many are formed without acknowledging that there is even a 'spiritual' side to humans, and certainly with no recognition that there is a God of impossibilities working in these kid's lives. I have appreciated and used a lot of the knowledge I gained in my teacher training during my ministry, and also in writing curriculum that is age appropriate, but I never want it to limit what God can do. I know at times I have been too heavily influenced by my training and by my conservative upbringing in the Church of Christ, and I am always striving to find the right balance.

Spurgeon says:

> *If you preach to the grown up people, to men of judgment, if they do not like what you preach, they can go elsewhere; but if you teach a child wrongly, he believes you; if you teach him heresies, he will receive them; what you teach him now, he will never forget. You are not sowing, as some*

---
[27] Ron Buckland, *Children and God,* Anzea Publishers, NSW, Australia, 1988, p. 55
[28] Joanne Brubaker, Robert E Clark & Roy B Zuck, *Childhood Education in the Church,* Moody Bible Institute, Chicago, 1986, pp. 14-15

CHAPTER 3 - THE GUIDE PICTURE

say, on virgin soil, for it has long been occupied by the devil, but you are sowing in soil more fertile now than it ever will be again... You are beginning with a child so take care what you do with him. Do not spoil him.[29]

I wonder many times how we only let the best speak to adults but often let anyone speak to the children. Shouldn't it be the other way around?

Spurgeon believed that teaching children when they were young was imperative. He highly valued those who work with children:

> *I wonder many times how we only let the best speak to adults but often let anyone speak to the children. Shouldn't it be the other way around?*

> Give us the first seven years of a child, with God's grace and we may defy the world, the flesh and the devil to ruin that immortal soul. Those first years, while the clay is soft and plastic, can go far to decide the form of the vessel. Do not say that your office, you who teach the young, is in the least degree inferior to ours, whose main business is with older folk. No, you have the first of them and your impression, as they come first, will endure last; oh that they might be good, and only good!.[30]

For Spurgeon, the call for "children to come" was clear:

> As soon as a child is capable of being lost, he's capable of being saved. As soon as a child can sin, that child can, if God's grace assist it, believe and receive the Word of God. As soon as children can learn evil, be assured that they are competent, under the teaching of the Holy Spirit, to learn about God. Never go to your class with the thought that the children cannot comprehend you; for if you do not

---

29 CH Spurgeon, *Spiritual Parenting*, Whitaker House, New Kensington, 1995, pp. 95-96
30 CH Spurgeon, *Spiritual Parenting*, Whitaker House, New Kensington, 1995, p.111

> *make them understand, it's possibly because you do not understand yourselves; if you do not teach children what you wish them to learn, it may be because you are not fit for the task; you should find out simpler words, more suited for their capacity, and then you would discover that it was not the fault of the child, but the fault of the teacher, if he did not learn. I hold that children are capable of salvation.*[31]

Jesus says that being a teacher holds a huge responsibility: "If anyone causes one if these little ones to sin, it would be better for him to have a large millstone hung around his neck and to be drowned in the depths of the sea" (Matthew 18:6NIV).

In his book *Children and God,* Ron Buckland says, "It's my belief that many people, including children, make decisions towards Christ. Rather than making a 'once-and-for-all' decision to follow Christ, I see the gradual steps into dawning light becoming that radical re-orientation of life called Christian Discipleship. God alone knows the point at which a person is saved. If we faithfully and carefully teach what it means to belong to God and the cost, we *are* evangelizing. Children can, and probably will, make decisions towards Christ as a result of our teaching."[32]

When we look at the life of Samuel, dedicated to God at a young age, we see he was immersed in serving and learning about God way before he even knew God. 1 Samuel paints a very interesting picture of how we should be bringing our children up in an active, serving environment where God can speak to them. Samuel was dedicated to God as a baby by his mother, even to the point that he was given to the temple priest to live and work there.

1 Samuel 3 says this about Samuel's experience:

> *The boy Samuel was serving God under Eli's direction...God called out, "Samuel, Samuel." Samuel answered, "Yes? I'm*

---

[31] CH Spurgeon, *Spiritual Parenting,* Whitaker House, New Kensington, 1995, p.111
[32] Ron Buckland, *Children and God,* Anzea Publishers, NSW, Australia, 1988, p. 51

here". Then he ran to Eli saying, "I heard you call. Here I am"...Eli said, "Son, I didn't call you. Go back to bed." (This happened before Samuel knew God for himself. It was before the revelation of God had been given to him personally)...Then God came and stood before him exactly as before, calling out, 'Samuel! Samuel!" Samuel answered, "Speak, I'm your servant, ready to listen"...Samuel stayed in bed until morning, then rose early and went about his duties, opening the doors of the sanctuary, but he dreaded having to tell the vision to Eli...Samuel grew up. God was with him, and Samuel's prophetic record was flawless.[33]

Samuel was ready to hear God's voice. He was serving and 'doing' things around the temple, long before God had spoken to him personally. It was all part of an important preparation for him and gave him a fantastic grounding. Just as a seed needs all the right conditions to grow, so our children's spiritual welfare must be taken more seriously.

As a parent, it's my personal dream that when God wants to speak to my kids they will be ready to hear and know how to respond. Just recently, my son, (whose name happens to be 'Sam' as well) came to me late one night after he had been in bed for a number of hours. He looked startled and said, "Mum, I think I heard God speak to me!'. My heart skipped a beat as I immediately thought of Samuel in the Bible. I said to Sam, 'Well, what did he say?". Sam said, "He was calling my name!" I replied, "Well go back to bed and if you hear it again, sit up and say 'I'm listening God.'"

He went happily off to bed and I didn't hear anything more from him. I was a little disappointed, thinking how exciting it would be if God brought him a clear word, as long as it wasn't a terrible message about his wayward family like it was for Eli and his sons! But, that didn't really matter in the long run. What matters is that Sam knows that God can and will talk to him, if he is willing to listen.

---

[33] Eugene H. Peterson, *The Message: I Samuel 3* ,Navpress, Colorado Springs, USA, 2002, p. 464

I have observed that many children are not seeing Christ make a difference in their life between the ages of 7-10. As a result, they are leaving the church saying that Christ has no relevance to them. You need to know what you believe if you are going to have a clear picture of what you are doing with the kids.

> **You need to know what you believe if you are going to have a clear picture of what you are doing with the kids**

If you believe that children should be seen and not heard, that they cannot make any serious decision until they are 12, and that they are under the complete responsibility of their parents until that age, then caring for them and making sure they have fun and are happy at church may be what your picture should look like. If your picture and theology of children is that they are innately sinful at birth and need to find a living, active relationship with God or they are going to hell, then just making sure they are happy at Sunday school won't be enough.

As an educator, I believe that unless we put our learning into action, we won't take it on board and assimilate it into our own life. I also believe that Jesus tells us adults to have the faith of a child, which would say to me that children have a special gift to offer the world that we need to rediscover within us. They have much to teach us and we need to empower them to act upon what they are learning.

It's important that ministry reflects the belief that children should put their faith into action. I always want to be involved in local ministry where there is kids' choirs, dance troupes, KIA groups, and Junior Leadership, etc., because this is what I believe is the BIG picture for us as ministers of children. Their faith must be active and God must be a part of their everyday life. Think of the process as creating 'reminders' for our children – reminders that build upon each other and eventually show them their own picture of Jesus that is real for them personally.

WHAT WILL YOUR PUZZLE LOOK LIKE?

It's so easy to go to another ministry and see what they are doing and be impressed. It's dangerous to go home and copy that! Sure, we can get great ideas from what others are doing, but remember that God has a vision and dream for the kids you work with and they are unique. You also bring gifts that are unique, and God will want to use them in your ministries.

We have Hillsong Church in Australia – a church that has inspired and changed the face of worship world wide. It's wonderful to go there, be inspired and worship God under the leadership of Darlene Zschech. But to go home and try to be Darlene would be the wrong thing to do. We are not meant to be someone else; we are uniquely made in the image of God. I believe that Darlene would be the first to say, "Find your vision from God, and do not copy someone else's." You can be inspired by what a church has done and you can find resources from other ministries, but your puzzle will be uniquely different to theirs. It must reflect the dreams God has given you for the community and church you and your team minister in.

George Barna believes children need to be taught the fundamental biblical principles and truths that underlie answers to their questions, but they also need to stretch their imaginations and envision personal applications in ways that transcend the recitation of stock replies.[34]

So, what will taking heed of this wise advice mean in practical terms for your ministry? For me – someone 'sold out' to making a difference for children in Australia – the journey of processing this with my own kids over the past 10 years has been revolutionary. My family is currently involved in a life-giving community. We have the simple mandate to grow "inwards through community", "upwards towards God" and "outwards to others who don't know Jesus". We have stepped away from traditional Church models and are on a journey as a family to what God is stretching us in.

---

[34] George Barna, *Transforming Children into Spiritual Champions*, Regal Books, Ventura, 2003, p. 70

For us, it has come out of a desire for Christ to be real and life changing, not only in our own lives but in our children's as well. So, when we come together to worship Him, everyone – no matter what their age – brings what they have to serve Him and each other. The children love it; we are all together and we are using our gifts. Although these are small beginnings, I have already seen growth and empowerment in my children and those we are connected to. This is our BIG picture!

 **WHAT DO YOU BELIEVE?**
(Take some time to answer this question for yourself)

1. Is your big picture the same as others in your team?

_____
_____
_____
_____

If you have a picture that isn't the same as everyone else's in your team, whether it's right or wrong, you will have a problem with unity and community, and there will be no sense of each moving in the same direction.

Only pieces from a particular puzzle can be used to complete it. The picture will never be completed if you are all using pieces from different puzzles. I feel this is a major issue for many ministries today, especially for those within larger church structures. Segmentations and departments have meant that there are pieces from many puzzles trying to fit within the one big puzzle.

Ministry can only function effectively if everyone is working toward the same big picture. If you find you are all building different puzzles, something must change or there will be division and disharmony around the corner. Conversely, there is nothing more exciting than being a part of a team where you are all on the same page. This can happen at all levels of the church.

CHAPTER 3 - THE GUIDE PICTURE

TEAM LEADERS AND CHILDREN'S WORKERS

If you are working in a large team, it's really important that the big picture for your ministry fits within the team leader's big picture. I have been part of a number of teams and found that this issue is pivotal to the success of God's ministry.

Andy Stanley talks about the need to be working together with your boss in his book *Next Generation Leadership*. In the local church, it's very important not to get so passionate about the children that you do not see that your vision must be going in the same direction as the whole church. Even if you think you are both going in the same direction, it's vitally important to communicate the vision. This is where you might find that your theology differs, which can cause problems if left unaddressed.

There came a turning point one year in local ministry for me where I realized that what I was passionate about was not in line with the senior minister's passion. I was asked to write down my goals and vision for the next year. When I presented what I felt God was calling me to do within the children's ministry, it was not the vision that my boss had. It doesn't matter who was right or wrong. I came to a place where I had to move on because I was not in line with where he was leading the church (the puzzle that he was creating) and I needed to get out of the way.

If your theology is different from that of your boss, then Andy Stanley would say that you are in the wrong place. "If that's the case, you may want to start looking around for another environment in which to invest your talents."[35] As painful as the process was, it was very freeing to move on and find a place that offered a better fit for me to serve. Obviously, the better solution is being able to communicate freely and make sure that you are working towards the same picture.

---

35 Andy Stanley, *The Next Generation Leader: Five Essentials for Those Who Will Shape the Future,* Multnomah Publishers, Inc, Sisters, 2003, p. 32

CHILDREN'S MINISTRY TEAM

No children's ministry works without a team, and a team needs to be working together. There are many ways in which you can find yourself differing. Varying beliefs in theology about children and how to minister to them is one area. There can be varying beliefs regarding discipling, worship and, in particular, teaching methods. I have had many a leader speak to me about someone who has been teaching the same way for 20 years and refuses to change and be more relevant to the kids.

> **The key to effectively and efficiently completing a puzzle is making sure the pieces are all connecting and working towards the same picture**

In the family of God we are all His creation, and while we may differ and struggle, we are supposed to be loving and caring and inclusive. I believe that the biggest struggle in team ministry is getting the whole team onto the 'same page'. In later chapters we will discuss ways to do this. It's important to know at this stage that if this is a difficult issue for team members, then ministry will always struggle. The key to effectively and efficiently completing a puzzle is making sure the pieces are all connecting and working towards the same picture. As I write this, I know that it's easier said than done.

SHARING THE PICTURE!

This is vital to making sure you are all working towards completing the same picture.

I hold a Vision Night at the beginning of each year. Anyone interested in finding out what we are planning for the Children's Ministry for the coming year is invited, and it is made clear there is no obligation to be involved. All parents are welcome, as I want them to understand what we are doing with their kids, and appreciate that we would be working in partnership with them in this whole mission.

The evening often begins by celebrating the past year's successes. I often tell many stories of children growing in their faith and serving God. Their stories are always so interesting.

For example, a parent told me that as the family was driving in the car one day, her 8-year-old asked her daddy if he was going to heaven. She proceeded to talk to him about heaven and how she would love to know that he would be there as well, as she loved God and was going to heaven to live with Him forever. She continued to tell him how to receive Christ in his heart, and she asked if he would like to pray about it. He listened with delight as she was very excited to share what she had learnt. When she finished, he assured her that he loved God too and was a Christian. Both parents were delighted that she understood so much and were really happy with the impact that the children's ministry was having on their child. Children's leaders need to hear these stories.

The Vision Night is always full of testimonies, and we often finish that section by all popping 'party poppers' or cheering so we could echo God's cheers in heaven as He watches His children growing in Him.

The evening then continues with an outline of the vision and goals for the year. The vision is always in line with the vision of the whole church. I always go over the vision any chance I get so people new and old may eventually get it. If you don't have a vision statement that people can remember and understand, then I suggest you need to start there.

> *If you don't have a vision statement that people can remember and understand, then I suggest you need to start there*

The goals change each year. They are the dreams and the new levels we want to achieve so that children can connect with Jesus in a stronger way. They need to be attainable, and yet dreams that also require faith and stepping out to see God at work. I may say to my team that we may not achieve everything, but when we dream and give it to God, we see Him work.

We finish with people being able to move around the room to take a look at the different ministries that are happening within the wider children's ministry for the year. They are given a chance to look at the job descriptions that are required for all workers, and to talk to key leaders about their experience. They leave with a form that they can fill out if they wanted to apply for a position; but if not, they leave with a clear message of what we are about. As a result of these nights the good word would continue to spread throughout the church of the exciting things that were happening in children's ministry.

This process would be the same for me with any ministry I would be involved in with children. I would do the same kind of thing for when I begin to pull a team together for a camp, a conference or a mission trip etc... Sharing the Big Picture can be so important for people to understand why we do what we do. People want to be a part of something that is going somewhere, has a set purpose, and a clear picture of what needs to be achieved.

 **ACTION STEP**

KIDS TALK

Video or interview some kids and record their answers to the following questions. This kind of process helps you know what the kids know and comprehend, and helps you understand where they are coming from.

Questions

Ages 0 – 4 years:

- Who is God?
- Where is God?
- What happens when you do naughty things?
- Who is Jesus?
- Where is Jesus?
- Can you talk to God?
- How do you talk to God?
- What is church?
- Does God love you? Why?

Ages 5 – 6 years:

- Tell me what you think of God?
- How old is God?
- What do you think God looks like?
- Who is Jesus?
- How do you know Jesus loves you?
- What did Jesus live on this earth for?
- What is heaven like?
- How do you talk to God?
- What is the Bible?
- What do you think God does when we do naughty things?
- What does God ask us to do?

Ages 8 – 12 years:

- Who is God?
- How can you be sure that God is real?
- How do we please God?
- What does it mean to be born again?
- How can God be everywhere?
- What is sin?
- How do you know that Jesus loves you?
- Why do you think you're here on this earth?
- What is the Bible?
- Why do we read the Bible?
- Who is the Devil?
- Who is the Holy Spirit?
- Why does God ask us to go to church?

The corner piece
Jesus must be our cornerstone
Your relationship with God is a vital piece of the whole plan

Putting together a puzzle is done more easily when you find the corner pieces first. They are the most solid pieces, as they have two straight edges each and form the framework of the puzzle. The corner piece shows you the context of the puzzle in relation to size and shape. It gives you a starting point.

Jesus has been described as the cornerstone of the building. Any builder will tell you the importance of the cornerstone to the stability of the building.

JESUS NEEDS TO BE THE CORNER PIECE OF YOUR PERSONAL LIFE
"See, I lay a stone on Zion, a chosen precious cornerstone and the one who trusts in Him will never be put to shame" 1 Peter 2:6NIV... God is more interested in you than in your ministry.

> *God is more interested in you than in your ministry*

Thirteen years ago, I went through a difficult time in my marriage. My husband and I decided to take a year off ministry and sort our marriage out.
I found the process difficult, for as I took one year off ministry I realized that my identity was wrapped up in being a children's pastor more than it should have been. Being very purpose-driven by nature, I found that doing nothing for a year and just learning to be with

God was a very hard thing to do. But it was the right thing to do. It is always important to put your relationships with those around you and, of course God, before ministry.

Just before we took the time off, I had to fulfill one final ministry commitment. I had said that I would speak and sing at a youth camp in Melbourne. I didn't want to do it, and felt like a fraud to be ministering when my personal life was in such crisis. As He always is, though, God was faithful, helping me each step of the way.

I remember finishing my commitments and sitting down as the group concluded with worship and ministry time. At this time, I cried out to God. I felt all alone in the darkness, not sure where to go next and feeling very fragile. I remember shaking all over, and feeling that God was embracing me. As I opened my eyes, someone was hugging me and praying for me. As I kept crying and shaking, I was scared but felt safe at the same time. I felt him saying, "You are my precious child, you are safe with me" over and over again. I spent a lot of time journalising that weekend, and left that time feeling a sense of peace I can't quite describe.

I returned home to the biggest family disaster of my life till that date, yet when it happened, all I could feel was peace. I remember sitting with a counsellor a few days later and recalling what was going on in our family and how I was handling it. He responded with a worried look. He said, "You seem very calm about this; are you sure you are alright?" I then described what happened on the weekend and what God had been doing in my life. He stated that God was actually preparing me for this event, and that He was giving me the strength I needed to get through it.

From that time on I have always been able to go back to that place where God and I can be together – where I learnt that being in His arms is all I need. Being His child had become the foundation of my life. I learnt that weekend that I can handle anything this world throws at me while ever I am His child. Apart from that revelation, the next most precious thing I gained from that experience was to see God work a miracle in my marriage. My husband and I are now in ministry together and that is a tremendous blessing.

"Whether a Christian leader builds a church or an organisation is ultimately not as important as whether he or she focuses on building a home... Never neglect your own family in your service to others"[36]

Gordon MacDonald, renowned author and speaker, said he went through a stage where he said to God, "I know that you're all that I have, but I am just not sure that I know you well enough for you to be all that I need."[37]

Mike Yaconelli, a well known writer, speaker and youth worker writes, "I had spent twenty-five years in church related ministry, and most of my days were consumed with writing, or talking about Jesus. And yet I was lost, consumed, soul weary, thirsty, and bone tired. I had succeeded at mimicking aliveness, but I was nearly dead."[38]

If we can learn anything from the journey of those we respect in ministry, it is that we must not keep going on in Christian ministry without Jesus being the cornerstone to every aspect of our life.

I am amazed at the people who serve God full time or part time and feel guilty when they take time out of each working day to spend time with God. If it is the only thing we do all day we would still be using our time wisely. The trap of ministry is that we spend so much time reading the Bible to prepare for lessons and teaching that it is the only time we read and study the Bible.

I have found when I am disciplined in my daily reading and time with God, not only are my days more productive, but more importantly the next step or great idea for ministry often comes out of what I am reading, studying and journalising with God. When we are too busy

---

[36] George, Hunter, Kennon, Callahan, Toler, *The Pastor's Guide to Growing a Christ like Church,* Beacon Hill Press, 2004 p. 47

[37] Gordon MacDonald, Speaker at *"Youth Worker's Conference",* San Deigo, Organised by Youth Specialties, USA, 1997

[38] Michael Yaconelli, *Dangerous Wonder: The Adventure of Childlike Faith,* NavPress Publishing Group, 1999, p.16

for time with God and reading our Bible, we are right where Satan wants us.

> **I press on toward the goal to win the prize for which God has called me heavenward in Christ Jesus**

"I press on toward the goal to win the prize for which God has called me heavenward in Christ Jesus." (Philippians 3:14NIV) It is God's desire that we all make it to the end. He wants us to see the completed picture. That means that we had better pace ourselves, realising that it is a marathon.

The statistics relating to how long people stay in children's ministry are frightening. As I speak at the same conferences year after year, I often ask who has been here before and for whom this is the first conference. I am always saddened by the many first-timers and the very few who have stayed on in ministry to children for a long period of time. That is not only sad for the children, it is sad for the many who crash so hard that they lose their faith in the process. The challenge for us all is that we don't become a statistic.

As I look back through my journals and quiet time reflections, I am amazed at how many times God has challenged me on new issues. But even more incredible is the way He is always preparing me for the next step, teaching me something new from the lives of many characters in the Bible. He is often preparing me for something down the track that I am not even aware of at the time. I am also amazed at the many times I get great ideas and new concepts that I often end up teaching and preaching about later down the track after God has dealt with me on the issues. If we don't spend that time with God, we will not stay fresh and growing in His direction. I love seeing things anew. When I read a passage that I have read before, it's inspiring to suddenly see it from another angle.

I often get into trouble for leaving rooms and facilities in less than perfect condition. Now, anyone who knows me understands that attention to detail is not one of my strengths. On this particular

CHAPTER 4 - THE CORNER PIECE

occasion, I had just finished a discipleship evening at a church and as I looked around the room, it seemed tidy to me. Everything was in place; there were a few papers on the floor, but that seemed okay. I locked up and went home, feeling it had been a great night discipling 40 kids and having a great time with them.

The next morning, I received an angry note about the papers on the floor and rubbish in the bins. The cleaner was very angry that she had to clean it up. Now, some of you might be thinking as I did, "I thought that's what a cleaner did! What is she getting so angry about?" I was quite deflated because I didn't understand what the fuss was all about. Whenever I go into a room I never complain about what has been left behind. It's a church. Countless people use it each day, and if something needs to be moved or picked up, I just do it and get on with what I am there for. (I can see some of you smiling... You know the drill: if there is something wrong, go to the children's ministry – they are sure to have messed up, right? We all know that is very common.)

Usually I get over it quickly and move on, but this morning I was feeling a little down because I figured the priority was supposed to be ministry, not how tidy the building was. At the time I felt like communication between staff seemed to be primarily about rooms needing to be spotless! I then opened up my daily reading and read from Luke 7. Jesus was having dinner with the Pharisees and when a harlot woman came in and anointed Jesus' feet, all the Pharisees could think about was "How dare he let her do that! Doesn't he know who she is?" Jesus answers so politely... And their response was priceless... "Who does he think he is....to say he can forgive sins?" They missed the whole point! Jesus is all about 'people' not 'procedures'.

Then it hit me. I mess up with the procedures many times because my priority is always the people. I miss the finer points and get into trouble, yet for the cleaners it seems to be all about procedures. I suppose that's because it is important to them that they do their job well... But at least after my quiet time that day I felt like I was in good company, and I could get on with the rest of the day without wallowing in the wrong things I continue to do.

> **If you can't think of the last time that you connected with Jesus, then it is time to stop reading this book and go and change that fact!**

Our time with God *must* be the source from which everything else springs. He must be our greatest teacher, instructor and inspirer. If you can't think of the last time that you connected with Jesus, then it is time to stop reading this book and go and change that fact! When was the last time God challenged or encouraged you directly? If you can't remember, then maybe you are not spending enough time with him and in His word.

Go directly to the source. Too many of us receive most of our input from books and great preachers. We must always keep that in balance as leaders, especially if we are to be a leader of leaders. Sometimes we find ourselves reading Christian books and not the Bible. Make sure you are finding the correct balance.

JESUS NEEDS TO BE THE CORNER PIECE OF YOUR MINISTRY.

Earlier in my ministry I had the privilege of hearing Bill Wilson speak in Australia. He was a children's pastor in New York, USA. I remember he was talking about having your 'own altar'. This was a place to go to when things start to get too tough, when people don't understand you and what you are called to do. I wrote down the notes of his message at the time, but didn't really understand what he was talking about.

But what was the big deal about an 'altar'?

I knew that God had called me – I will always remember the moment. I had just finished my third year at teacher's college. At that time, I was offered the opportunity to undertake a fourth year to complete my degree. It was a great opportunity, and taking it up would have really pleased my dad and my husband (the two most important men in my life). Becoming a teacher would have been seen as more prestigious than ministry, and it certainly would have meant earning more money. (Of course, if you knew me at all, you would know that money means very little to me. This was a real frustration for my accountant husband at the time!). But I was really struggling with being a teacher in the school system. I wanted to work with kids, but I wanted to teach them more significant things than maths and spelling. I know they are important things, but I wanted to teach them about something that is life changing, not just life enhancing.

As I was pondering what to do, I heard about a warehouse in Sydney that sold craft supplies for kids clubs. When I got there, it was certainly filled to overflowing with crafts, but more important still, I learnt about the vision behind the warehouse. A man named David Young had started an outreach to kids and had made an impact on thousands of Australian children. I am not much into crafts, but the kid's club idea really excited me.

I drove home, my mind going wild with ideas. I remember thinking, "But how can I do all that if I go back to college next year?" That was a moment I will never forget. I felt a very strong voice inside say to me, "I want you to make a difference for children in Australia for me!" My heart was beating. I didn't know what to do next, and so I did what any girl does when they don't know what to do... I went home to Mum. (Well, maybe not everyone does that, but it's what I did!) I went to the one person who has always taught me that I could do "anything I put my mind to". She is my mentor, and now, in later life, one of my closest confidants.

I sat down and told her what I felt God was saying and she simply listened and said, "Go for it!" That was 1989, and since that day I have been sold out for ministry to children. No matter how difficult things get, no matter how confusing the direction is, no matter how misunderstood and alone I have felt, that call has always kept me standing strong. It was the 'altar', Bill Wilson had spoken about. There are times when it is the only thing that has kept me going.

There have been a number of stages in my ministry where I have been through diffi cult times. It is then that I've realized that the 'altar' Bill Wilson was talking about is imperative. When you face hard times, you had better know that Jesus is the corner piece in your ministry and in your life. I have learnt the importance of being called by God and having a vision from Him. Until that decisive event in the car that day, I had simply enjoyed working with kids. It was the thing I was doing at the time. But that pivotal moment has proven crucial to me lasting in ministry for this long.

> **Until the heart of the leader is right before God, the works of the leader will ultimately be ineffective**

"Until the heart of the leader is right before God, the works of the leader will ultimately be ineffective"[39]

JESUS NEEDS TO BE THE CORNER PIECE OF THE MESSAGE

He is the reason we do anything. Everything must centre on Him. All that we do should come from Him. This is a life commandment. It is sad to see George Barna's observation that in American culture today, while this should be a given, Jesus is more of an 'add on' for many.

Even on a Sunday, other things can take away from Jesus being the centre of the message. What message are we giving our kids? Could it be:

- Good Christian kids sit quietly and never interrupt me when I am telling a story.
- Being a Christian is about behaving well, saying the right things and looking respectable.
- If you remember the memory verse you will earn a prize.

---

[39] George, Hunter, Kennon, Callahan, Toler, *The Pastor's Guide to Growing a Christ like Church,* Beacon Hill Press, 2004, p. 35

- The program is about catching up with friends that you don't get to see all week.
- I will talk to you in this group time, but when it is over, I am talking with the adults; please don't bother me.
- If we accept Jesus into our heart, our life will be wonderful from that time on.

For too many Christians, Jesus is not central to daily life, but rather the thing you do on a Sunday. It is just not part of the postmodern ethos to live for someone else. To live with Jesus as our starting point – active in every part of our life – is altogether foreign to this generation. There are not many places where children are going to go and find someone putting someone else higher than themselves.

This is why the concept of 'worship in music' is so foreign to our kids. They know all about idol worship and hero worship. Hero worship means we want to be like someone else. We worship our heroes because we admire a skill, or their money, or their looks. To worship a God whom you can't see, or to worship a God who doesn't promise you gold and riches or an easy life is a new thing altogether. No earthly hero calls you to say you are a sinner – or asks you to accept him as Saviour. To worship a music idol or sports idol means to be entertained, or get pleasure out of watching them play. To worship God in our daily life is to honour Him for who He is, because He is God. We need to clearly model this lifestyle, showing children that life with God really gives them a hope beyond tomorrow. They will never grasp the sense of purpose they can receive unless they understand it is centered on Jesus.

JESUS NEEDS TO BE THE CORNER PIECE OF OUR PUBLIC LIFE

Jesus needs to be central in our life, and it needs to be evident to those around us. We need to be a walking, talking testament that Jesus is central to our lives. This of course needs to be an outward reflection of our personal life.

The greatest thing you can do for your children's ministry is stay close to God. Having been in ministry 'officially' for 20 years, I am beginning to see the amazing and scary impact you can have on children.

Children's leaders don't like to hear this but, from 0–6 years of a child's life, you are God to them. I mean this in the sense that you are a walking, living example of God to these kids. They see what you do, and it reflects God and the way He treats them. Then as they grow older and they are looking for role models in the faith, you become someone they admire, emulate and copy.

> **The greatest thing you can do for your children's ministry is stay close to God**

I can't count the number of times a child has said to me, "When I grow up I want to be just like you." I have learnt that it is not that I am anything great; it is the nature of the age to want to have heroes. I have a sign on my desk that has a child looking up to the sky, and saying, "When I grow up I want to be just like you". This is *my* prayer: to be like Jesus in everything I do. I am reminded time and time again that I always have growing to do.

The responsibility is huge. As I look now at those I held up as heroes when I was young, I find many of them are no longer in ministry, have lost their faith or have fallen in some major way. Where have all the good guys gone? Of course, as we grow we learn the reality that we are human and we do fail, and it is only the grace of God that keeps us in the faith. But we are challenged by God to finish well. As I have matured in the faith, those heroes of mine that have fallen have not affected my faith, but the reality saddens me and urges me to fight the good fight, to complete the picture that God has created me for and serve Him faithfully to the end.

At a dress up night a number of years ago, we had a 'Come as Your Dream' theme. I came as a rock star (a dream I've had since I was a child). I had the glitter in my hair, the glam jacket on and wore big silver high heeled boots. For me, any chance to dress up is fun!

A 10-year-old girl walked up to me, with a microphone in one hand and wearing three-quarter pants and a nice, simple, colorful top. She said, "Guess who I am?" I went through a few of the rock stars that the kids like, but she shook her head to them all. I eventually admitted defeat. "I give up," I said. Smiling, she looked at me and said, "I came dressed as you!" I was taken aback at first, and then in embarrassment said, "Wow...you need to dream a little higher than that!"

We don't like to admit it, but they are watching carefully and mimicking. So we must stay on track. I watched a whole ministry go down the drain and many children leave the church shattered when our youth pastor was charged for being a pedophile 15 years ago. We have a huge responsibility. What we say on the outside must reflect what we are on the inside. It must be real and genuine. Otherwise you can be sure "your sins will find you out".

If you are a volunteer in ministry, it is even more imperative to make sure that preparing for a lesson is not the only time you are reading the Bible. What we teach and model for the kids should come out of our own life's experience. Not many weeks go by when I don't use an example of something that happened to me that week as I speak to children on a Sunday. If we are to model faith to our kids, we must show them that Jesus is a living, active person in our daily lives.

When my son Sam was 6, he sat in the back of the car on a day trip and asked Georgia (my then 3-year-old) if she loved Jesus. When she said yes, as all 3-year-olds do, he continued to say, "But have you asked him into your heart?" Of course Georgia said, "What does that mean?" He opened the Bible that was next to him and started from the beginning, taking her through five key stories in the Old Testament. He then took her to the New Testament, to Jesus dying on the cross, and gave her the Gospel message right there and then. My husband and I kept our faces to the front for fear of interrupting, and with tears in our eyes, listened to Sam lead Georgia to Christ.

As a pastor, you always fear the 'Pastor's Kid's Syndrome', and we are nowhere near past it yet. But it brought a sparkle to my heart that he had learnt something from us that excited him about Jesus and the need to share about Him. Our kids should benefit from our ministry, not be burdened by it. If we can't live it with them, we won't be able to teach it to others.

> **Our kids should benefit from our ministry, not be burdened by it. If we can't live it with them, we won't be able to teach it to others**

I want my faith to be so real and passionate that my kids and those around me 'catch' it and want to connect with God more and more. Jesus is the author and model of this kind of living. The Bible says there was something about him that attracted people to him. People followed him and listened and watched everything He did.

Jesus must be the corner piece of both our private and public life, and the central theme of what we teach the children we minister to.

 **TAKE SOME TIME OUT WITH GOD**
(Take the time to write your answers)

Jesus needs to be the corner piece of your personal life:

1. How is your personal life with God? What is He teaching you at the moment? When was the last time you let God change something in you?

   _____
   _____
   _____
   _____

2. What are you reading in the Bible at the moment? What Christian book are you reading at the moment? Do you have a good balance between reading the Bible and reading other Christian materials?

   _____
   _____
   _____
   _____

Jesus needs to be the corner piece of your ministry:

1. Do you remember a time when God challenged you about children and working with them? If so, take the time to write it down. If not, then think about what you are doing working with kids! Are you there for the right reasons, or are you intending to move on one day to bigger and better things?

   _____
   _____
   _____
   _____

Jesus needs to be the corner piece of your message:

1. What is the message you are giving to your kids through your messages and teaching?

   _____
   _____
   _____
   _____

2. Are you sure that Jesus is the centre of everything you teach?

   _____
   _____
   _____
   _____

Jesus needs to be the corner piece of your public life:

1. If the kids you are ministering to came to your home, would they see the same person they see when you are in ministry with them? What would be different?

   _____
   _____
   _____
   _____

2. If there was one area in your public life that didn't stack up with your private life, what would it be and how can you take active steps to work on that?

   _____
   _____
   _____
   _____

The vital edges
1: LEADERSHIP

You cannot build a strong ministry framework without positive leadership

The edges of a puzzle are for building the foundation of the puzzle. They help enclose all the other pieces, and then form the framework for a finished and firm puzzle. When you don't have the right edges, you immediately know that something is missing. They are important to put in place first, to establish the strength in the puzzle. The vital things that make an effective lasting ministry are leadership, team building, understanding the community's needs (the kids and the families that you are working with) and having a solid discipleship process in place. No one aspect is more important than the other, but there is a planning process when establishing a ministry and because of this I believe leadership must come first.

I believe that leadership is one of the biggest problems with children's ministry today. I would go so far as to say that unless we address the issue of the lack of leadership in our ministries, we will not see a major change from this generation to the next generation.

There are three reasons why I believe we have major issues in leadership.

1. CHILDREN'S MINISTRY IS NOT VALUED WITHIN CHURCHES

We are still fighting an attitude that says children's ministry is something you do while you are learning about ministry, and then when you have finished training you can be a 'real' minister or have matured enough to work in 'real' ministry.

I was interviewing for an intern position a couple of years ago and one of the applicants actually wrote on the form that he is called to youth ministry but hoped this opportunity would help put him through college and give him some great experiences. While I admire his honesty, he was lucky to even get an interview with me. Children's ministry must move beyond a training ground for youth pastors. Don't get me wrong, I am not putting down youth ministry. It is a vital ministry. It is important to simply stress that they are very different ministries, requiring different knowledge and skills.

Children's ministry is still a role that is primarily undertaken by lay people, part-timers, or a youth pastor on top of everything else he/she has to do. While ever children's ministry doesn't have a paid person on staff to do it, it will never be taken seriously. Most other ministry positions in the church require qualifications of some sort. Why shouldn't ministry to children be the same?

Valuing children's ministry more highly has to come from the top down. George Barna says that churches where the children's ministry prospers are those led by pastors who are unapologetic advocates for that ministry focus. They represent its best interests in strategic meetings, budgeting and staffing decisions; they keep their eye on the quality of church activities offered for the children; they celebrate victorious progress; and they communicate its importance in sermons and presentations to the congregation. "As a personal observation, I believe that if the pastor does not include the ministry to children as one of the top church priorities, the chance of that ministry reaching its potential and having a significant impact on the lives of the church's children is severely damaged"[40]

2. LEADERSHIP AMONGST CHILDREN'S WORKERS IS NOT VALUED

In Australia, I would call this the "She'll be right" attitude – the "near enough is good enough, after all they are just kids" attitude. However, it can be seen in any country.

As I took time out to write this book, I was reading a book on leadership as part of my research. I was by the pool as my kids were swimming at a wonderful resort hotel in Orlando, Florida. (It's a hard life...Hey, while mum is working it is important that the children are happy!) Let me take you there, too. Picture the scene. Just as I am reading and processing through the importance of leadership, an employee comes out and calls all the kids who want to play some games to come to the side of the pool. My son Sam is right there – he'll grab any chance to play with some other kids. This guy has about 15 kids around him - all strangers to each other. He then chooses the two biggest kids of the group and says, "Right, pick your teams!"

Now, I'm thinking, "I can't believe this guy is doing this!" This is breaking the basic rule of how to get kids into teams in a positive way. Then he watches as the kids fumble through, having no idea who to pick or what they are even doing. I sit there – as a mother, uncomfortable for my son who gets picked last because he's so small, and angry as a children's worker because this just doesn't need to happen. The kids play around in the pool then, while he tries to give instructions. Ten minutes later, he's given up talking and just says, "Go!" The kids scramble for eggs in the pool. They bring them back but have no idea what team has what pile. It's a total mess. Then once all the kids have come back, he gives a big cheer, then picks two more captains and gets them to choose a new set of teams for the next game. This is agony to watch.

---

[40] George Barna, *Transforming Children into Spiritual Champions,* Regal Books, Ventura, 2003, p. 105

He explains the next game, but then he turns away to get something. By now, his teams are falling apart and going off to swim – they're sick of sitting around and waiting. He starts the next relay, and kids are being knocked over by other kids swimming. Many kids are cheating (they don't know the rules), and as a result, the other team wins (the team that my son is not on). Now, the "That's not fair!" part of me kicks in. By the final game, the kids start to get it together; they have a fun final relay game. (This time my son's team wins). The employee thanks the kids and leaves.

Now the wonderful thing about kids is that they are forgiving. They simply got on with swimming and having fun, now with new found friends. But if you can't see the things wrong with this picture, you are going to be in big trouble when you are trying to lead a group of kids to do something they don't really want to do. Sure, this was an employee at a resort just entertaining some kids beside a pool for a while. But if he were with adults, they would not be impressed with the haphazard way things were done, without any professionalism or leadership skills.

> **The first thing I ask them is, "Would you do this with a group of adults?" If the answer is no, then don't do it with kids**

The fact is whenever someone is leading a group of people – large or small – they are in a leadership position. Whether you are leading some games or leading them to Christ, you are still leading. You can choose to do it well or have a "near enough is good enough" approach. I have seen too many children's workers just do an average job, because "they are just kids". They do things with kids they would never consider doing with adults. The first thing I ask them is, "Would you do this with a group of adults?" If the answer is no, then don't do it with kids.

We need to take leadership with kids seriously and do the best job possible.

3. CHILDREN'S LEADERS ARE OFTEN THOSE WHO LOVE CHILDREN BUT HAVE NO LEADERSHIP SKILLS

This has been a hard reality for me. I learnt a few years into ministry that if I was going to see the children's ministry grow, I had to become a leaders of leaders and let others do the ministry to children. It was something I resisted for a long time.

I remember the first years of ministry and how keen I was to work with children. I needed help, but I didn't care about the leaders. I only cared about the children. There were many times when people felt like they had no idea of what was going on and probably felt used by me as a leader. I had the best interests of the kids in mind, but the leaders just had to do what they were told.

I learnt very quickly that children's ministry is not something you can do on your own. You need a strong team and many workers, and you must lead them. I love being with kids. I miss doing stuff one on one and in small groups with children week in and week out. I believe that God called me when I was 20 to "Go and make a difference for children in Australia for Him". That is my life commandment

> *children's ministry is not something you can do on your own*

– the statement that guides all that I do. Therefore, if I was going to lead a ministry of 250 kids and 70 volunteers with 2 interns and 1 administration assistant, I had better understand that my role is to empower other leaders to do the work, find strengths in others, and communicate well to everyone. Otherwise, those children would not be ministered to effectively.

If you are reading this and think, "Well that's okay for you Tammy. That's a big ministry. I only have 20 children; I can do it all myself." Well, let me tell you, if you want the kids to grow, if you want them to bring their friends and for them to grow, you had better start building into leaders' lives. As a leader, we are there to empower others to serve Jesus. I am currently in a small life community with

20 children and 50 or so adults, and the issues remain the same; size is irrelevant. We are building the team for outreach and growth.

It seems to me that when God wants to make a difference in the world He calls a leader to bring about that change. He called Jonah to bring a new message to the people. He called Abraham to make a new move to a new country. He called Moses to set His people free. He called Paul to talk to a new culture. He called them all to lead and bring about change. If we are going to see a change in children's ministry, it is going to happen when leaders begin to lead with a purpose in our children's ministries, rather than simply be people who love kids and are happy to be there to look after them.

When I ran a *Friendzy* discipleship program for kids aged 8– 12 years, while the team was building, I had to fill in the gaps until I found the right people to do all the jobs. This meant that in the early stages, I had to run the games, prepare the food and clean up. I would have much preferred discipling the kids. I would have dearly loved to get in there and just nurture a few kids; but that would have meant only 7 kids would be discipled. This way, 50 kids got discipled, and I had to run the program and work with the leaders. We must be a leader of leaders if we are going to see children's ministry grow. My time must be spent training, communicating, recruiting and empowering others in the ministry or it will be stunted in growth to what ONE children's worker can do with a small bunch of children.

There was a time when I felt frustrated that while the kids were in their small groups, I was driving out of the premises to get chips for the meal; times when I was setting up for the next session while the leaders were spending quality time with the kids. I was thinking, "I should be doing that!"

Then a thought came to me: "The difference between leadership and being a team member is that the team member lives in the present and the leader lives in the future".

For me at the time, it was a profound thought. It made sense and I suddenly understood why things were going so well. If something is going to grow and develop, it needs a leader who can keep his/her eyes focused on where he/she is going and keep one step ahead of the team, trusting the team to do the "in the present" ministry with the kids. It was a releasing thought for me. I was feeling so frustrated, as though I was missing out. But when I saw it this way, I was released to keep on dreaming and planning ahead for where the team and kids could be travelling.

So if you are reading this and feel, "That is too hard" or "I just want to be with kids and play with them and talk to them about Christ", then I would say to you, "Go for it!" But, you will need to leave being the leader to someone else and you can be a part of the leadership team.

> **The difference between leadership and being a team member is that the team member lives in the present and the leader lives in the future**

I have often felt that way. I used to love being part of a leadership team on youth camps when I was young – just to be with a small bunch of kids for a week and get away from the responsibility of being the leader. I could play up, muck around, and simply hang out with the kids. But I knew in my heart I was called to leadership, and that means foregoing the thing I love most in order to see God's plan come to pass. Don't misunderstand me – I love envisioning, planning, empowering others, and seeing kids growing in Christ. I love what I do. But I have come to understand the sacrifice of leadership.

I believe we need more people in the role of children's pastor or team leaders that understand leadership. I would rather see someone in this position who has leadership skills and can build a team than to see the best puppeteer or storyteller in this position just because they love kids and are great with them, despite having no idea how to empower others to do their best.

THE STRENGTH OF LEADERSHIP

Working with children today is not easy. It is a known fact that getting people to be involved with children's ministry is not always easy. I believe strong leadership is a way to help this growing problem. Now, the word 'strong' can mean many things and this is not the book to go into details about what strong leadership entails. There are many fantastic books out there that can help you understand strong leadership in the right context. But let me explain a little about some elements that I believe are important.

LEADERS NEED TO BE ABLE TO LEAD OTHERS ON A JOURNEY

People want to be a part of something that is exciting. When leadership is strong and inspiring, people want to get involved. You are recruiting out of strength and excitement, not weakness and need. It is important to have a vision and a plan. The next step is to be able to communicate it positively to those around you.

> **When leadership is strong and inspiring, people want to get involved. You are recruiting out of strength and excitement, not weakness and need**

You cannot lead people where you have not been. There is no point trying to be something you are not. People can spot a phoney from way off, and if the adults can't, the kids surely will. This does not mean that you have to have it all together, but you need to have a sense from God of where you are going and to be able to encourage and inspire others to want to go on the journey with you. You need to be someone who is living it daily with God. Leadership is a huge responsibility.

It is important to stress that it doesn't mean you know *everything* ahead of everyone else. I think of Moses leading the people out of Egypt. All he knew was that God said "go". It is not easy pioneering something new, but leadership is a key to any new pioneering experience. We are asking people to follow God, and God is using not only you as a leader but those he gathers that are with you at the time.

LEADERS NEED TO BE ABLE TO EMPOWER OTHERS IN THEIR GIFTS AND ABILITIES

Those of us in leadership need to be positive, encouraging, and people who can allow others to use their gifts for God even when they will do a better job than you. Within this environment, people will flourish.

I have had people on teams who would never have thought they would work with children in ministry, but they wanted to be a part of a winning team that is making a difference in the community. As a result of using their gifts, they have grown to love children and see the value of what they are doing to advance the Kingdom.

Does this mean that you are willing to accept people who have never worked with children? Or even worse, don't *like* working with children? Let me give you an example – one of the musicians on my team. He is a fantastic musician – a jazz and blues guitarist. I believe in getting the best for the kids in all areas, so I asked him if he would help me write some songs for kids. He said he would love to. We began writing songs; he began playing them for me with the kids. He had never worked with kids before and would never have thought of doing so; he wasn't confident enough. But he can play the guitar. He had struggled to find a place in the church to use his gift; he didn't quite fit in. So he was happy to be finally using his gift for God.

As he began to play for the children, he was amazed at the children's response. They loved to worship God, dance and sing, and get involved. It was the most fun he'd had in church for a long time. He has stayed ever since. He loves doing what he does for children and being a part of a team that encourages each other, works together, has fun, and sees kids grow more and more in love with God through worship in song. This was all because I asked someone to use his gift with kids and join a winning team that brings fellowship and meaning to his life. I am frequently asked why the best musicians in our church work in the children's ministry. I say it is because they can use their gifts for God and they feel empowered to do this.

LEADERS NEED TO BE WILLING TO TRUST THAT GOD CAN DO MORE THAN WE CAN CONCEIVE

I run a camp in September of each year and have a team that I pull together to help me to begin dreaming in July. One particular year I laid out the plan for the theme of the camp and we dreamed together about what we could do if we had no boundaries. (Of course money is always a boundary, and my accountant always gets worried when I start dreaming!) We called this theme the 'Game Master'. It was based on popular card collecting games such as *Pokemon* and *Yu-Gi-Oh!*. The kids love to collect the cards and swap them. I wanted to see a set of cards developed especially for the week, and be able to provide all the kids with a set. I also wanted to put them into a life-sized maze, which would put them into a situation where they had to put the learning into action; this is where they would earn their 'Level 2' card.

The entire team's heads were spinning after the first meeting, and I don't know if half the leaders even grasped the concept until they had finished camp! But as we started working it through, it became apparent that finances were not going to allow us to pull it off.

At the final meeting with the whole team (about 60 leaders), I shared the dream and the ideas again, together with the need for us to pray for a miracle to get these cards. As I was speaking, a new leader seated at the back raised his hand. He said, "I'm a graphic designer. Could I have a look at the ideas you are thinking about?" A cheer went up in the crowd of leaders. "Of course you can," I said. "Let's talk after the meeting." Then another person's hand went up, and he said, "I work for a printer. I'm sure if I talk to them about what we are aiming to do, he would be willing to print off one set per child for free"...

Well, my heart leapt and we finished the meeting by thanking God for answered prayer. What seemed impossible only weeks before was now possible! The camp was a huge success and the kids loved the cards, which were pivotal to the message about the vital things we need to live life well. It would have been so easy to say, "That's a great dream but we can't afford that", and move on. Within all our goals we must leave a little room for God to move. People want to be a part of a team that dreams, and is led by someone who leads by example when it comes to relying on God and believing for the impossible.

These are only two of the many stories I can tell you of how positive leadership and building a strong team can make all the difference to children's ministry. It is not only a vital key, but you cannot grow or have a stable, positive framework without it.

> *Within all our goals we must leave a little room for God to move*

SOME PERSONAL QUESTIONS TO THINK ABOUT REGARDING YOUR LEADERSHIP:

1. What are you passionate about when working with your kids?

2. Are you at your best when you are the leader of adults or part of the team?

3. Where are the gaps in the leadership of the ministry you are involved in? Take time to ask God about filling the gaps.

The vital edges
2: COMMUNITY NEEDS
Understanding the community we live in is vital to being effective in ministry

KIDS AND THEIR FAMILIES

This is often overlooked as a vital piece of the puzzle, and yet the reality is that without children and their families there would be no ministry. In fact, we need to shift our thinking quite considerably when it comes to understanding that ministry to children has to be done within the context of the family.

For too long we have segmented adults and kids and forgotten that this is a created concept from the institutional Church model, not necessarily God's design. Not only are we to find ways to empower parents to spiritually raise their children, but to help families as a whole unit find out how Jesus can make a real difference in their lives. This is a two-fold mission; we must help support the growth of families that know Jesus, and reach out to the families that do not yet know Him.

TO EMPOWER 'CHRIST-CENTERED' FAMILIES WE NEED TO:
- Encourage parents to spiritually train their kids
- Find ways to bring families together
- Help families to become healthier within

It is vital to be on the cutting edge of the needs of the families in your community who do not know yet know Christ. There are a number of ways to keep in touch with the community's needs:

- Talk to the people who live within the community
- Live within the community
- Understand the trends for this generation
- Understand child development and what the basic needs of children are for certain ages

Let's look at these areas in more detail.

WE CAN EMPOWER 'CHRIST-CENTERED' FAMILIES BY...
Encouraging parents to spiritually train their kids

> **Parents are God's first curriculum**

"Parents are God's first curriculum."[41] We need to understand that our children are most influenced by their parents. Surely our focus needs to be on how best to support and equip parents to bring up their children with a spiritual worldview. These are important issues for the future of the church and for children's ministries everywhere. I believe that we need to focus more on families as a whole, and less on kids in isolation from the family. Taken seriously, this will radically change the way we do ministry in the future.

While I have felt strongly about this for a long time, I hadn't conceived what that might look like until I went to North Point Community Church in Atlanta, Georgia in the USA. What I witnessed there was like seeing a long-held dream become reality, and it escalated my passion to see this change within our local ministries.

North Point Community Church's then Children's Pastor, Reggie Joiner, believes that families like to do things together. They go to the

---

[41] Brubaker, Robert E Clark & Roy B Zuck, *Childhood Education in the Church,* Moody Bible Institute, Chicago, 1986, p. 11

movies, theme parks, the beach and football games together – why not go to church together?[42]

Reggie believes that God has ordained parents to spiritually grow their children. We see that the children's minister has an average of 40 hours per year to spend with a child compared to the parents' 3000+ hours a year with that same child. Parents therefore have the most potential to influence children.

> **Parents therefore have the most potential to influence children**

As a result, North Point Community Church spends a significant amount of time and resources on encouraging and empowering parents in their role as spiritual teachers. North Point runs a *KidsStuf* service where the kids take their parents to church. The *KidStuf* services are dynamic and relevant to the family – everyone learns the same biblical principles, together. The parents are equipped with take home packs that include music, stories and thought provoking questions designed to initiate family discussion wherever the family may be together, be it in the car or at the dinner table.

The children's worker's focus then becomes empowering and supporting parents and guardians in their God-given role as their children's spiritual teachers, as opposed to simply trying to do their job!

Finding ways to bring families together

I believe one area of relationship-building that we need to look at for the future of the church is how we involve the family unit. This does not mean that we define the family, or make a judgment on what a family is. More importantly, we embrace everyone as part of the family of God and look at helping all types of families in whatever place they find themselves. North Point are already well on their way along this journey.

---

[42] Reggie Joiner, *Founder & CEO The reThink Group - Alpharetta, GA*, www.kidstuf.com / 252basic.org

When I talk to parents, most agree that bringing the family together is what they want, but they openly admit that they just don't know how to start. We need to assess the programs and ministries we provide for families and determine if they largely break them up or bring them together.

Part of the journey our family has been on within our current life community is finding ways to be together. We try to organise events and moments where families can enjoy being together and serving God together. Of course, it requires more work and is not for everyone, as I have discovered that a number of parents really don't like being with their children. But for those who do, we need to start thinking about how that might look.

McDonalds in Australia has made it really easy for the whole family to go and enjoy the family dining experience. It has been a deliberate move on their part to make sure that there is something for everyone. Now our whole family can enjoy going to McDonalds. My husband can have a nice coffee, I can have a real cup of tea and reasonably healthy salad or 'deli choice', and the kids can have burgers and chips. The adults can sit in nice lounges and enjoy a drink and something to eat while the kids have a great time in the playground. It is a 'family experience'.

How can we learn from this and help the family enjoy God's presence together, learn together, pray together? This question is vital to connecting with this generation and the current needs of the family.

Our family has had the joy of being in ministry together; whatever we do in ministry we do together. When I am speaking or teaching somewhere, my kids and husband are often doing drama or music or something like that with me. These have been wonderful, genuine experiences for my children, helping them see that Jesus is active and real. Whether it is involvement in mission trips, helping at a camp, working in the neighbourhood, caring for a family, or worshipping and learning together, I guarantee that you will be surprised by the possibilities if you change your mindset on the importance of doing it together.

Helping families to become healthier within

We need to look at ways that we can help improve relationships within the family, equipping them with the tools to bond together. These days, the church is expected to take full responsibility for children's spirituality, yet this is totally unbiblical. Research also shows that churches generally register the children into a program, teach them, and then show little interest in contacting the families or working with them in any way, suggesting churches must take responsibility for perpetuating the problem.

"Churches who tell families that the church can do spiritual formation better are usurping what I believe to be a parent's God-given responsibility and gift: to care for the souls of their own children. They are taking on a responsibility no program can ever fulfill."[43]

The Bible is very clear on the role of parents in the development of the spirituality of their child. Passages like Deut 1:31, 6: 4-9, 11:18-21 and 21:18-19, as well as Ephesians 6:4 show clearly that parents should provide the primary spiritual training for their children. Parents are encouraged to work together with reliable spiritual partners such as the church to make sure their kids are committed to the things of God (1 Sam 1: 27-28). Isaiah 7:15 and Acts 26:4 state that parents must start spiritual training of children at a young age.

So how do we embrace this current need? We must look at whether we are encouraging parents to take a key role in teaching their kids spiritually. I fear that if I list ideas that it again will limit the possibilities. However, short courses and suggesting creative available resources can be a start. But principally it requires a change of mindset, and I have found that providing opportunities for families to do things together helps the mindset to change.

Once you see the impact it makes on a child or a parent to feel they can make a difference, the possibilities are endless.

---

[43] Ivy Beckworth, *Postmodern Children's Ministry: Ministry to Children in the 21st Century Church*, Zondervan, Grand Rapids, 2004, p. 106

In our life group one time, a family provided some supper. Their 4-year-old had helped with the cooking of the supper and announced that if we wanted to eat what she had prepared we had to pay $1.00 per cake, as the money she raised was going to help her sponsor child. From little beginnings, those parents are helping their daughter understand the greater need in the world and how she can make a difference. Focus on the Family has many resources to equip and give ideas. We need to be a part of changing the mindset and help empower parents to grow together.

HERE'S HOW YOU CAN BE AT THE CUTTING EDGE OF THE NEEDS OF THE FAMILIES IN YOUR COMMUNITY WHO DO NOT YET KNOW CHRIST…

Talk to the people who live within the community

People often ask me how I know where kids are at. The simple answer is I talk to them and I listen to them. I hang around with kids and their families. Yes, it means in some sense I am never 'off duty'. I have discovered many things at a local Under 7's football game, while at Playmaze with my preschoolers, or when I'm shopping. It can take time, but the more we immerse ourselves in the community we live in, the better we are going to understand that community's kids.

> **We must be able to talk to people without them always feeling like we are trying to convert them. They need to see that we really care.**

It is also important to realize that if we are serious about being a strong foundation of truth in our community, the community wants to see if we are a part of the community. I think it is an insult when we live separately from the community we are yet trying to connect with. We find it offensive when people don't listen to what we have to say, yet so often we don't take the time to listen to them. Jesus called us to "be in the world and yet not of it" (John 17:15-18). Too many Christians have very little to do with people who do not know Christ, and then wonder why we are not relating to our community.

When I speak at conferences about the world our kids live in I am amazed at what children's workers don't know about this current culture. We must be able to talk to people without them always feeling like we are trying to convert them. They need to see that we really care. They need to see that we are actually interested in listening to what they want to talk about.

Live within the community (incarnational ministry)

It is vital for us to be immersed in our local community. If we are going to impact this generation, we need to be involved in all aspects of community living. It is one thing to minister to the Christian kids in your community, but they are only part of the picture. There are many families and children out there who still need to hear the Good News. It does help having children when you are ministering to children because there are countless ways to be 'Jesus with skin on' – volunteering at the canteen, for example, or offering yourself as a parent helper in the classroom to listen to children read.

The saddest part about being in full-time ministry is that ministers rarely have contact with people outside of church. I have found it is vital for me to have non-Christian friends, to play community sport, to teach Scripture, to help out at the local school, and to be involved in community events. People are more interested in how you can help them rather than what you can tell them.

> ***People are more interested in how you can help them rather than what you can tell them***

One of my favourite Australian speakers calls this 'incarnational' ministry. Michael Frost believes that if we really are going to connect with our community we need to reject the attitude that if we put on a good children's program, the children will come to us! People in our communities need to "experience Jesus on the inside of their culture". If we are to break into the culture we live in we must be a part of it.

For most of the people who live in our community, becoming a Christian is synonymous with becoming a somewhat happy but bland, usually white, almost always middle class, middle-of-the-road kind of person. As Michael Frost says, "This kind of person is exemplified by Ned Flanders in Matt Groenig's immensely popular and insightful cultural critique, The Simpsons."[44]

I'm reminded of an experience I had when I went to 'Biker's Week' in Daytona, Florida. Around 30,000 bikers come to Daytona during this week, and they basically take over. I had never seen so many bikes in my life. We drove around surrounded by bikers. The noise was amazing. It was an incredible experience, and an amazing visual spectacle. Bikers do have a 'look' about them and a style that is unique. We obviously didn't fit, but that was okay. I remember seeing a church as we drove along. It appeared closed – not a sign of life anywhere – yet a notice out the front declared: "Tonight – Youth Rally – 7.00pm – Free food and drinks – All Bikers Welcome!" I couldn't help but wonder if anyone turned up that night! That image reminded me of just how often we Christians miss the point about being 'in' the world and yet not 'of' the world.

In stark contrast, we were recently having the deck at the back of our house repaired because it was falling down. A builder from our church was helping us do it. He brought his non-Christian son over to help us for the day and we all had fun laughing and working together. We were just being ourselves, and had some great conversations – some serious and some downright silly. (If you knew my husband you would understand that was an understatement! He is fun and lovable, and people thoroughly enjoy being around him.)

At one stage during the day, my husband dropped something on his hand and expressed himself. (He swore; not a really bad word, just one that expressed his pain at the time.) The builder's son's response

---

[44] Michael Frost & Alan Hirsch, *The Shaping of Things to Come: Innovation and Mission for the 21st Century Church,* Strand Publishing, Erina, 2003, p. 40

was, "I didn't think you would be able to say that!" We all laughed. The next day our builder friend came to finish the job and said, "Thank you for yesterday." We were a little dumbfounded as he was doing us a favour. We asked him what he meant. He said, "Jamie really enjoyed yesterday. He has such weird ideas of Christians, he couldn't believe how normal and fun you were! It was a great witness to him."

We underestimate the witness we can be in community with others. Unfortunately, because most things happen inside church, "God becomes mute to the majority of people in the western world."[45]

Understand the trends for this generation

This is so important to complete the right puzzle for your ministry. We are complex people and you can never stop reading, watching and learning on this topic. I watch all the kid's shows and movies that come out. Even when I didn't have children I would take my cousins to the movies – and not just for an excuse to go to a kid's film. It's one thing to see the movie; it's another thing to see it 'with' a child. I remember a number of years ago going to Disneyland with a group of youth leaders. After about 3 hours they wanted to leave because they were bored. But just this year I went with my two children, and two days just weren't enough! Everything is different through the eyes of a child.

Frost and Hirsch indicate that people today are looking for a sense of belonging, empowerment, sensuality, and celebration. If this is so, consider whether our kids experience any of these through our ministries.

Hugh MacKay observes in his book *Reinventing Australia* that Australian families feel alienated in a world of so many choices – that children feel a sense of hopelessness in the future.[46] When is the last time you read something about the trends of the future? When we read them, how do they impact our ministries? I can't read any of these statements

---

[45] Michael Frost & Alan Hirsch, *The Shaping of Things to Come: Innovation and Mission for the 21st Century Church*, Strand Publishing, Erina, 2003, p. 40

[46] Hugh Mackay, *Reinventing Australia: The Mind and Mood of Australia in the 90s*, Harper Collins, Melbourne, 1993

without seriously looking at what we are doing in children's ministry. I ask the question, "Are we really scratching where kids are itching?" Echoing George Barna and Leonard Sweet, I would have to declare, "No, we are not."

> ...fewer than 10% of parents who regularly attend church with their kids read the Bible together, pray together or participate in an act of service as a family unit. In short, most families do not have a genuine spiritual life together

George Barna states that "fewer than 10% of parents who regularly attend church with their kids read the Bible together, pray together or participate in an act of service as a family unit. In short, most families do not have a genuine spiritual life together."[47]

What have you read lately? What has challenged you in recent times about how we might be doing things differently in the future? When was the last time you went to a conference and heard something new that challenged your way of thinking? When is the last time you had a conversation with other key leaders about how you can improve on ways to connect with your kids? If you can't answer questions like these, I challenge you to start to think about how serious you are about connecting kids with Jesus as opposed to simply running a 'good program'!

Understand child development and the basic needs of our children at various ages

There are many books available for you to read that clearly describe the development stages of children and describe in detail the key elements our kids are dealing with at particular ages.

Here is a brief outline of the developmental stages of a child:

---

[47] George Barna, *Transforming Children into Spiritual Champions,* Regal Books, Ventura, 2003, p. 78

- 1 – 4 years: Discovery
  (What happens when I put my hand on that?)
- 5 – 8 years: Testing
  (How far can I go? Why?)
- 9 – 12 years: Concluding
  (Knows everything)
- 13– 14 years: Discovery
  (What happens when you do this?)
- 15– 17 years: Testing
  (Why can't I stay out late?)
- 18 – Onwards: Concluding
  (Knows everything)

We need to understand our children's development at least at a simple level. This way we can make good decisions about what we teach them, when we teach them certain truths, and understand why they are behaving in certain ways.

Many parents talk to me about their children, worried about why they are behaving in certain ways. You need to be able to help them in these areas, or guide them to places where they can seek help. Sometimes it can be a simple issue of understanding their development stage.

I had one parent speak to me recently. She had a son who was 5 years old and always dressed as Batman or Spiderman. He was a lively kid, but not destructive. (Personally, I would have described him as just 'creative'). She came to me extremely worried – concerned that he always wanted to be a superhero, always wanted to run around and save things, kept flying around the house... She was embarrassed when he dressed up, especially when he insisted on wearing his superhero gear when they went out in public.

I was able to put her mind at ease immediately by assuring her it is normal for 5– 6 year old boys to want to be a superhero, to save the world, to want to dress up and pretend. I encouraged her to make sure that he was able to be himself at times when it was important like meal times, or when he needed to be doing something for her, to make sure that he wasn't escaping from life in general for any reason. She felt sure that he was fine in all those areas, it was just something he liked to do a lot and she had been worried about it. You can imagine her relief at discovering this was all part of being at his particular developmental stage, as well as being reflective of his personality and probably even his learning style.

Sometimes we can squash highly creative kids because we are personally embarrassed about what they are doing. It is something that we need to be aware of as teachers, leaders and parents. Children will do things that embarrass us that we would never do and will even behave in ways that we would have never imagined. Does this necessarily make it wrong? Is it just a stage, a phase, or an important learning period for them? If you know the characteristics of children at their different stages, you understand how best to meet those needs at the time.

Compiling a study of your community provides you with a better idea of how to serve them. I have found keeping up with trends, reading constantly and talking and living amongst those in the local community is a full time job. However, this is what I believe we are meant to be all about if we are to be truly mission-minded and able to reach out effectively to our community. This is not only a vital part of my calling as a minister, it is also a requirement of anyone who truly wants to connect with a group of kids and make a difference in their lives for Jesus.

The edges build a framework for everything else that fits in the puzzle. Knowing and connecting with the families and children you minister to will also set the framework for what the final picture of your ministry will look like. Take some time out to design the appropriate picture with which to minister to the children within your Christian community, and 'outside' in the community around you.

ACTION STEP

- Plan now when you can take some time to do some study to learn more about the age group that you minister to.

  _____
  _____
  _____
  _____

- Talk to others (even some kids) about what is going on in the world of kids today.

  _____
  _____
  _____
  _____

- Take a morning out and spend some time with your team reflecting on the effectiveness of what you are doing. Celebrate the success and pray about the ways you might be falling short.

  _____
  _____
  _____
  _____
  _____

PIECE BY PIECE - TAMMY PRESTON

CHAPTER 7

The vital edges
3: TEAM BUILDING

Ministry will be as strong or as weak
as the team we work within

It is really important to take the time you need to build a strong team. And it does take time. We can cave in to the pressure of running things with a 'shoe string' team, especially if a particular ministry has been running for a long time or parents want a certain program to happen.

When I took on the role of children's pastor at a particular church there was a *Kids Klub* operating. Just three leaders were running the program, with about 50 children attending. Prior to starting in my new position at the church, I went to visit so I could observe how it was run. I was shocked at the program's lack of quality – all because there was such a limited team. The three who were there were doing their best, but I could see that the amount of organization required to deal with such large numbers of children was slowly killing three good leaders. The entire program had the potential to be 'taken over' by the children. Sure, it was a lot of fun, but was that what it was all about?

Two months before I started, the parents got wind of the fact that a new children's pastor was coming and that *Kids Klub* may be closed down. I started to get pressure from the parents about what I was planning to do. A band of parents emailed me with a proposal that involved them running it for the next two months until I got there to take it over so that it could remain open. The pressure was on.

> **I am all for outreach, but not at the expense of poor leadership and overwhelmed teams**

I am all for outreach, but not at the expense of poor leadership and overwhelmed teams. This was one of those cases where it would be all too easy to fall into the trap of reacting out of need. As Jesus said, the need will always be there (see Matthew 26:11). I gently wrote back explaining the importance of strong teams and healthy programming and that until I could start at the church and begin to see what teams of people I had to work with in the ministry, it was good timing for *Kid's Klub* to have a break. I also added that when I arrived, if they wanted to talk to me about being involved in the ministry I would be happy to talk to them. It wasn't the popular decision, but it was the right one. *Kids Klub* never started up again, and none of those parents ever joined the ministry team. It is also important to note that the three leaders running the club were burnt out and had a long break when I started there in ministry. There is much to learn from this example.

As team leader and builder, it is important to:

- Never run a program/ministry without a solid team, no matter how 'good' the ministry is.
- Be careful not to burn out good leaders by asking them to take on too much. It is your job to protect and care for them.
- Never give in to parent pressure if you feel it is the wrong direction for the ministry. Even though we are there to serve the families, it is not to be at the expense of quality ministry.
- Do not fill places with people who are doing it out of a sense of duty or for the wrong reasons.

- Pray about any new move in the ministry – for God's timing and provision. He will provide for the needs if it is the right direction to go.
- If someone approaches you to start a new ministry, ask questions about their reasons for wanting to see this happen.

BUILDING STRONG TEAMS

How do we build strong teams? Effective ministries have a recruiting strategy that includes clear job descriptions. They only accept people who feel they are called to the ministry, and they provide training and support. Ministries that have done this with respect to team building have found recruiting successful.

Effective ministries develop great team leadership. This is true of any ministry; it is just a new concept to many children's ministers.

Training leaders professionally and regularly is also a key to effective teams.

Below, I have outlined some strategies that I have found helpful in recruiting and maintaining the teams that I have led. While many of the examples I am giving are based in the local church, please note that they are principles that can be used right across any ministry organization, no matter what it looks like or how it is structured.

CLEAR VISION

People want to be a part of something that they can see is written down and verbalized very clearly. They want to be a part of a team that has a clear direction and has goals that can be evaluated and celebrated when they have been reached. This way it is very easy for people to see that they are a part of a team that is going somewhere and that is serious about its purpose. This builds a sense of 'team'.

Aim at today and you will get caught up in the daily and miss the mission. Aim at tomorrow and you will hit the mark of God's high calling

"Aim at today and you will get caught up in the daily and miss the mission. Aim at tomorrow and you will hit the mark of God's high calling."[48]

If I were to give two people water guns and ask them to take aim, you can bet you would know where they would aim. It would either be at me or at each other. If I took people to an archery range and gave them an arrow and bow and said, "Just shoot!" we could be in big trouble. We don't do that, do we? We tend to give people a target to aim at if we are going to arm them with a weapon.

So often we put people in positions of leadership – we even arm them with a curriculum and/or resources – and then say "Just shoot!" We then wonder why people get easily distracted, why people don't last long in a position, and why people tend to begin blaming each other. Just as two people armed with water pistols end up shooting at each other, workers who don't really know what they are doing likewise end up blaming each other when things go wrong.

An aim is a simple thing. Mission and vision have been talked about extensively over the past ten years in the Christian world, yet I am amazed at how many ministries are yet to have an aim or vision. If they do, the workers often have no idea what it is.

THE BODY CONCEPT

Corinthians 12:12 clearly states that we are all given gifts and a place to serve in the body. One of the major problems in children's ministry is that we are expected to be good at everything. All this does is make children's ministry a place where people don't want to serve because the expectation is so high.

I know the things that I can't do well, and if I am forced to do them, it will either force me to quit or it will be a mess and I will feel like a failure. If I am required to organize or administrate we are all in trouble. We inevitably end up meeting at the wrong time, on the wrong date, in a place that doesn't exist or isn't booked! My team,

---

[48] Leonard Sweet, *Carpe Mañana: Is Your Church Ready to Seize Tomorrow?*, Zondervan, Grand Rapids, 2001, p. 16

the children and their parents all applauded when I finally got an administrative assistant to help out in the ministry at one church where I was working. Now they would finally know when meetings were really on, and where they would be. We could finally know when kids attended, when they were away, and when their birthdays were.

In any given ministry there is a range of gifts required. The body concept recognizes that we all need each other's different gifts. There are some people that remember birthdays and some people who don't, there are some people who can cook and some who can't, and there are some people who are visionary and some who are great with details. We need them all. It was a great relief for me when I realized that God does not ask us to be able to do everything brilliantly. It has also been a great relief to others that I am not asking them to join the team and be able to do everything brilliantly.

There's a wonderful children's story I love to read to my kids called *Edward the Emu*. It is about an emu in a zoo that listens to what people are saying as they walk past his cage. When he hears someone say they like a particular animal best, he slips into their cage and tries to act like that animal so he can be noticed. He tries to be a snake, a tiger, a seal and some other animals. He tries so hard to be like everyone else. Eventually he hears someone say that it is the emu that they like to see. He can't believe that all the time he has been trying to be someone else, there have been people coming to the zoo especially to see him. That night he hops back into his cage to find to his surprise that another emu has taken his place. As Edwina the Emu turns around to look at him, she says with a shy little smile, "You are by far the best thing that I have seen since I've come to this zoo."[49] Edward is finally happy to be himself. There is nothing more satisfying than finding just the right place in the family of God, where you can fit and serve just the way God made you.

The body concept means that I ask people to work *only* within the area of ministry for which they are gifted. In this way, someone can come and be a part of the *Caring Team* and know that they will never

---
[49] Sheena Knowles and Rod Clement, *Edward the Emu*, Harper Collins, 1988

be expected to set up a craft, to sing a song up front, to tell a story or work with a puppet. They come to care for a small group of kids, to get to know them and to play with them. This is such a great way to get many different people involved who would otherwise never work with kids. People say to me, "I can play with a kid, but what's the point? That's not very helpful." Then I am able to show them that one of our core values is relationships. It is the key to the way we do discipleship. What you do by playing and caring for five children is imperative to how we achieve our goals for this ministry.

> **All have different but important purposes, but people only have to work in the areas for which they are gifted**

People can choose to be in the *Creative Edge Team,* the *Caring Team,* the *Arts Team,* the *Active Team,* the *Teaching Team,* or the *Technical Team.* I have called this the 'CCAATT System' to make it easy for everyone to remember. Using this system ensures people work within their teams and feel a strong sense of identity within them. All have different but important purposes, but people only have to work in the areas for which they are gifted. This builds a team in an important way. People feel empowered in the areas they feel comfortable in, and the children experience a depth of leadership and a variety of people types involved with them on a weekly basis.

JOB DESCRIPTIONS

Each person needs to be given a set job, and the expectations of that job are to be clearly spelled out for them. This ensures they know exactly who they are responsible to and who they are responsible for. They need to know what is required of them so they are aware of the number of hours expected and the spiritual gifts necessary to undertake the role.

At the beginning of each year, I would often put the job descriptions out for all to see at a meeting. Potential leaders were able to read them and decide what position they would like to take up for the year.

Once they nominated a position, we would talk about it and 'sign off' on this job together. This way there were no surprises; they knew what they were signing up for and knew what was expected of them.

LIMITED SERVICE

I believe that many people don't want to serve in children's ministry because they are scared they will get stuck there and will never escape again. I ask people for a year's commitment. This is because the ministry is largely run through relationships. I believe this cannot be done successfully in less than a year.

At the end of the year, at a break up party, I literally 'fire' everyone. That way they don't feel obliged in any way to return or do the same job. I make a joke of it and enjoy firing them, but of course this is preceded with a whole lot of encouragement and celebrating of the good things that have happened throughout the year. I also make a statement that goes something like, "Thank you for all that you have done, and for the amazing ministry that has happened because of you being involved. I have loved working with you and would love to work with you again next year. But I officially fire you because I want you to know that there is no obligation or guilt trip if you want to have a break".

Everyone has six weeks' break and is invited to come along to a vision night at the beginning of the next year for a no obligation look at what is happening that year in children's ministry.

QUALITY TRAINING

This is something I believe we don't focus enough on when it comes to kids generally. In the workplace, you need different degrees of training to do a job. Even within the church, a volunteer wouldn't think of running a Bible study, lead worship or even try to make a good coffee in the café without some degree of training. Yet, often we have no difficulty putting adults and younger people into a situation with kids without any guidance at all.

Working with children is getting harder; many people will not consider volunteering in this ministry because of the fear of being thrown into the deep end with a group of kids who will run rings around them. It is one of my pet peeves about parenting. We would never consider being a teacher or a doctor or a builder without some training, but the number of adults who will go into parenting without any knowledge of children is frightening. No wonder families today are struggling with how to stay together and how to bring up their children.

Training must be an essential part of the ministry. I know that it is hard to get people to take time out of their busy life to come to training. This is where you need to make it worthwhile. I have found that when I put effort into making the training exceptional, leaders come. Once they have found it a worthwhile use of their time, they will make it a priority to come again.

You might like to consider the following ways to make it worthwhile for your leaders to attend.

- Hold the training somewhere else to get away from the usual setting. It makes it exciting, and God is able to work in different ways when we are taken out of our comfort zone.
- Connect with other churches or training in the area. There is much to be gained by being part of a bigger crowd and meeting with people doing a similar ministry in other churches.
- Bring in a guest speaker to train your people. I know that it will frustrate you to pay someone to say what you have been saying for the past six months, but trust me – your people will take it on board because someone else has said it. Suddenly, they will see it for the first time and they will own it! That's when change can occur.
- Food is always a good way to attract people – good food and good fellowship.
- A cost needs to be involved. People often feel that if something is for free, it is not worth attending. They might feel if they don't turn up they won't miss anything. Being required to pay for it, however, makes them more committed; they come with an expectation to gain something.

- Make it a priority to get away with your KEY leaders once a year. Take them somewhere special, to a great conference out of town, for example. There is so much to be gained by spending time and money on these people. Take them out of their comfort zone and see what God will do.

INVEST TIME IN PEOPLE

This one is a challenge for me, but I have learnt the hard way that people need to be treated like people and not merely as job-fillers. I am very task driven, and while that might achieve a lot over time, one soon learns that people will not stay working with you if they don't feel cared for.

I remember asking everyone in the middle of a meeting, "What would help you work better as a team?" Their response amazed me. They said that they would like to make some time to socialize together and get to know each other better. Well, in my mind, I was thinking, "I can't even get you to these meetings half the time, and now you want to make more meeting times?"

I went along with the plan because that is what they wanted, and by the third social event I began to realize that this was actually making a difference to the work environment and the way they were working together when they ministered together on a Sunday. Running a ministry for kids is often time consuming, and when you are in the middle of it you very rarely get to ask the people you are working with, "How are you going?" I began to make a point of getting to know my team on a personal level that did not involve ministry. We started to care for each other and become friends.

This is not always easy. You may not become the best of friends with all of the team, but you start to appreciate them for different things. I had been aware of the saying, "The family that plays together stays together", but I had never applied it to the work situation. And let's face it, ministry should be more than a work situation.

I discovered the time I spent listening and caring for other people was time well spent, even when it meant that nothing was ticked off my list for that day. I began taking my 'core' team (there were four of them at a time) on 'out of the box' experiences. (I learnt this from Craig Jutlia, Children's Minister at Saddleback Church.)

The rule was that we were not to talk about work or ministry, and we were to just have fun. They didn't know where they were going – it was a little mystery – and that was always intriguing for everyone. It was just plain fun and it began to cement our team; we began to work better together.

> *I discovered the time I spent listening and caring for other people was time well spent, even when it meant that nothing was ticked off my list for that day*

PROMOTE AND EMPOWER

It is really important to be always thinking of the future and how to see the best in everyone. We all want to grow and try new things. It is sad when you see someone doing the same thing for ten years; it is as if they are stuck.

Now, I must clarify the above. I mean doing the same thing the same way for ten years. I have been in ministry for over twenty years. I'm still working with kids and will always do so. But I have grown and changed in so many ways that I am not the same person I was twenty years ago.

Always challenge people to do something new, even if it is within the same job. Training and going to see other ministries in action can certainly assist with this, along with reading and research. My role as a leader includes finding ways that my team can grow and be stretched. Some will naturally thrive and grow more than others. That's okay, because we all have different purposes and gifts. The key for us is to make sure that people are growing where they need to. This means allowing people to fail, giving them opportunities to be in a safe place, and debriefing with them when things don't go as well as planned. Even when someone feels they will never do something again, the experience is never void of learning something. Often it is only during the experience that we can truly learn new things. When is the last time you challenged someone on your team to do something new?

This might also mean that you need to be willing to give away something you love doing, which is especially hard when someone else does it better than you. You need to be secure enough to know that when you empower someone to do something new, you are actually fulfilling your role as a leader. I used to joke about doing myself out of a job, and over time I actually did in a number of areas.

I love to lead worship; it is hard for me to hand it over to someone else, but that is just me being selfish. I had an intern who had a gift in this, and after some time being with me, it was obvious that she needed to be empowered to fly. I allowed her to take over a whole service. She led the worship, did the teaching and ran the team. After a while I would sneak to the back of the room where she was ministering and watch as she led the kids brilliantly. How exciting to think that I had the maturity to let her have a go and not hold onto it myself. I missed leading at times while sitting up the back and watching her relate to the kids so well. But I knew that that was what was required of me as the leader of the team.

It is important to empower others in their gifts and enjoy watching when they begin to bloom. If you can't build your teams beyond your own ability then you have no business being a leader of leaders, and you will always struggle to keep good, strong people working with the children.

If you can't build your teams beyond your own ability then you have no business being a leader of leaders

ENCOURAGEMENT AND SUPPORT
I must confess, this is the last strategy
I have listed, not because it is the most important (although it probably is), but rather because I completely forgot about it in the first draft of this book. I tell you this because often we think that people who write books must do it all well.

Encouragement and support is something I have to work hard at. I am the person who never remembers people's birthdays or people's names, and even when I say I will give a prize out at the end of a lesson, I forget every time. Of course the children never do, and I always feel so slack about it. I love people, but I am not good at details.

It goes without saying that we need to encourage people, and especially kids, to be intrinsically motivated, but in all honesty, every one of us likes to be encouraged and told we are doing a good job. There are many ways to do this, but of course the most powerful way is to come alongside someone personally and tell them how much you appreciate what they do.

I am amazed at how many people feel they never receive any encouragement, and how easy it is to make someone's day. I remember one day when I put in the church newsletter a little thank you to our bus driver for driving the bus faithfully every week. He was a quiet man, happy to be in the shadows, content to just drive the bus. He walked up to me with the paper in his hand and tears in his eyes and, said, "Thank you". It was all he could get out, but I realized that day we don't encourage people in the simple things enough. He drove that bus for many years after that. I know it wasn't because of that article in the paper, but the little encouragement he got along the way would have made a huge difference. This is especially true for people who feel that what they do goes unnoticed.

There are many ways in which we can encourage our workers and they don't have to be complex. It can be as simple as a card, a spoken word in private or public, an article placed in the church newsletter, an award, a special dinner, a care package, or a small gift. Perhaps they could even be given a break. It doesn't need to be much, but it can go a long way to building strong teams.

These are some of the most effective ways I have discovered to get people involved in ministry and to solve issues with regard to recruiting hard to find volunteers. Team building is such a vital edge that it can make or break a ministry. It needs to be solid, and strong as a foundation to the picture you are trying to create for effective ministry.

 **PERSONAL ACTION STEP**

1. Reflect on your vision for your ministry. Do your leaders know what it is? Do you and your leaders know it off by heart when asked?

   _____
   _____
   _____

2. Does your team have a clear idea of your expectations and a clear understanding of the ministry that you are asking them to undertake?

   _____
   _____
   _____

3. What would be a positive next step for your working relationship with your boss/adviser/pastor? Are you communicating more positives or more negatives about what is happening in your ministry?

   _____
   _____
   _____

4. Are your expectations realistic for your whole team?

   _____
   _____
   _____

5. If you worked on the body concept, how could you break down the ministry into areas where more people work within areas where they utilised their gifts only?

   _____
   _____
   _____
   _____
   _____
   _____

6. Take some time to think of three simple ways that you could encourage your team in the next ten weeks.
   1. _____
   2. _____
   3. _____

7. Plan a social event where people can relax and enjoy each others' company! (Remember the rule: no ministry talk)

   _____
   _____
   _____
   _____
   _____
   _____

8. Who can you think of in your team who has been in the same position for a long time? How can you empower them to stretch themselves and try something new?

   _____
   _____
   _____
   _____
   _____
   _____

CHAPTER 8

The vital edges
4: DISCIPLESHIP

The purpose of the ministry is to introduce children to Jesus; therefore, we need a deliberate process of growth for our kids

If we have come to the conclusion that Jesus is the corner piece and that the purpose of the puzzle is to not only introduce children to Jesus, but to see them grow more like Jesus, then discipleship has to be a vital aspect of the puzzle. It should be a core value that we spend much of our time and energy on.

I was standing in the line at the post office and there was a lady with a baby in front of me. The people in the line were admiring the baby and fussing over it. Then one lady said, "Isn't a shame that they grow up?" and everyone agreed! I didn't. I felt weird about that comment. I thought, "Why do we not want them to grow up?" I know we all like babies; we think they are cute, sweet, lovely to cuddle, controllable, small and easier to handle... I could go on. But it began to dawn on me that it is in our nature to want our kids to stay young, immature, totally dependant babies.

Yet so much of this thinking is a fantasy, not to mention unbiblical. Babies are not easier, they are different. Many times you are guessing what they need, they are constant and exhausting...Yes, they are beautiful – but not without their own challenges. The reason it is an unbiblical concept is because we are not meant to stay on milk all our lives.

> By this time you ought to be teachers yourselves, yet here I find you need someone to sit down with you and go over the basics on God again, starting from square one—baby's milk, when you should have been on solid food long ago! Milk is for beginners, inexperienced in God's ways... Hebrews 5:12-13[50]

> *Our children are getting to the age of 10 and feeling that they have never tasted anything interesting enough to continue to explore the meat of Christianity*

Imagine the world full of babies: we would achieve nothing, make nothing. Maybe life would be simpler ....But fulfilling our true potential? No – otherwise God would have designed us to remain babies.

This brings me to the next issue that the statement in the post office raised for me. Why are we still treating children like babies – only giving them milk to feed on, never letting them sharpen their teeth on meat and taste the wonderful and wide selection of food that our taste buds enjoy? Could it be because we are still drinking milk ourselves?

I believe this could be true because I very regularly see the following things happening:

- Young people and adults cut their teeth in children's ministry, and then when they mature they move on to other ministries.
- We are singing songs with kids we sang 20 years ago. That's like eating the same food for 20 years. Every day!
- We keep to the simple things because we like the thought of innocent babies. It spoils it for us when we have to get serious.

---

[50] Eugene H Peterson, *The Message: The Bible in Contemporary Language,* NavPress Publishing Group, 2002

CHAPTER 8 - THE VITAL EDGES - 4: DISCIPLESHIP

- Our children are getting to the age of 10 and feeling that they have never tasted anything interesting enough to continue to explore the meat of Christianity.

There is no doubt that babies are innocent and beautiful. They make us smile, and we love to be with them (when they are not screaming or smelly). The challenge is for us to help them keep their innocence as well as grow and learn more so they can fulfill their purpose in Christ.

WHAT, THEN, IS DISCIPLESHIP?

"Spiritual leadership is simply assuming the responsibility to help your kids advance in spiritual growth"[51]

"A disciple means learner"[52]

Discipleship is a lifelong journey that one takes with Jesus. It is never too early to start and never too late to stop. I feel very privileged to have had an upbringing that meant I don't remember a time that I was not 'in love' with Jesus and desired to serve Him.

> **Discipleship is a lifelong journey that one takes with Jesus. It is never too early to start and never too late to stop**

I grew up in a Christian home, and while for many that is a negative, for me it was a positive. My journey with Jesus began when I was a baby and has kept on growing. I have the same desire for my children as well. As I write this they are 8 and 11 years old and they have always said they loved Jesus and He is part of their daily lives. I believe they have begun their journey. My role in the discipleship process is to continue to help them to grow, to help create experiences and opportunities for them to see God actively involved in their lives. Discipleship is not something you can define, not something you can easily plan, not even something

---

[51] Reggie.Joiner, Speaking at *"Children's Pastor Conference"*, Altanta, USA Founder & CEO The reThink Group - Alpharetta, GA, 2004,

[52] Michael Breen and Walt Kallestad, *The Passionate Church: The Art of Life-Changing Discipleship,* Cook Communications Ministries ,2004, p. 35,

you can test; but that doesn't mean that it is not real. Discipleship is certainly a life long process.

I am convinced that discipleship needs to be a vital focus. In fact, I believe it is the key to reaching this new generation.

> *Those who make up the next generation of believers are disoriented. They don't just want a map, they want a life coach. We keep offering them new maps – worship experiences with dimmed lights and candles – when they are crying out for a personal guide. This generation, perhaps like none before it, is desperate for discipleship. The essence of being a disciple is spending time with the teacher himself. And that is just what we get as followers of Jesus – an invitation to his home where we can hang out with him, listen to him, have him listen to us and become friends.*[53]

> ***...your spiritual condition by the age of 13 is a strong predictor of your spiritual profile as an adult***

We can achieve this goal in a variety of ways.

We need to begin as young as possible. George Barna concludes that "your spiritual condition by the age of 13 is a strong predictor of your spiritual profile as an adult. It seems clear that a deep and robust spiritual life demands intentional and strategic spiritual nurturing during the early childhood and adolescent years."[54]

If we are serious about impacting our society and nation for God, we must look seriously at what we are doing with our children. George Barna suggests that if we want "to have significant influence on the development of a person's moral and

---

[53] Michael Breen and Walt Kallestad, *The Passionate Church: The Art of Life-Changing Discipleship,* Cook Communications Ministries , 2004, pp 27-28

[54] George Barna, *Transforming Children into Spiritual Champions,* Regal Books, Ventura, 2003, p. 41

spiritual foundations, we had better exert that influence while the person is still open-minded and impressionable – in other words, while the person is still young."[55]

It is important that we understand discipleship is not about waiting until they have publicly 'confessed Jesus as their Lord and Saviour;' rather, the process of discipleship starts a lot sooner than that. The greatest gift we can give a child is a foundation upon which they can live their life, and that best foundation is Jesus. But for that foundation to be solid, it needs to be established and acted upon from an early age.

We must understand that our children gain nothing from a whole lot of head knowledge without them seeing its relevance to their daily lives. This is the main reason why children walk away from God as soon as they can. This is no different from the way I disregarded algebra once I finished school. I never saw any further need of it in my teenage or adult life. I still don't. It is sad to think that so many people do the same with Jesus, considering he has all the answers to life.

THE PROCESS OF DISCIPLESHIP

I was challenged by a minister that I respect a great deal when he asked us a question that he was asked years ago by a man that he, too, respected. Alan Meyer, Senior Minister of Careforce Australia asked me, "What is your process of growth for those that you minister to?"

> **What is your process of growth for those that you minister to?**

It was a great question and a challenging one. As I thought it through, it made sense that we have a process we are aware of, especially if discipleship is a vital edge to our ministry. That the process may be different for every ministry is not the important thing, but rather that you actually have one.

---

[55] George Barna, *Transforming Children into Spiritual Champions,* Regal Books, Ventura, 2003, p. 47

To take it a step further, his question also challenged me to think about my personal process of growth in important areas of my life such as spiritual growth, marriage, parenting, personal health and so on. I have always been someone who is very goal orientated, so I tend to write my goals for the year in all these areas of my life. I place them somewhere where I can read them regularly, and they help me to stay on track and make sure that I am growing in all these areas. You can only be as effective in other's lives as you are effective in your own.

Alan's question led me on a quest to define and streamline the ministry I was involved in at the time. I am fearful that spelling out what worked in the local ministry that I was involved in will encourage people to simply copy it. You need to work this through for yourself to make it fit with the ministry that you are involved in. But the principle will remain the same for any ministry.

THE SIFT PRINCIPLE

Let's look at the key essentials of the growth process for our kids. Alan Meyer used four key words: Knowing; Growing; Serving; and Sharing.

- Knowing: To know Christ as Savior
- Growing: To grow as a child of God
- Serving: To begin serving others with the gifts God has given us.
- Sharing: To talk to others that are 'not-yet' Christians about who Jesus is.

This is a very simple yet concise process. I wanted to be able to make it so simple that even the kids we were ministering to could understand and remember it. The SIFT principle was born.

As I have explained previously, the vision statement we had outlined for the ministry that I was involved in was:

CHAPTER 8 - THE VITAL EDGES - 4: DISCIPLESHIP

*'**S**aved by Jesus*
    ***I**ntended for growth*
        ***F**or serving others*
            ***T**o share the good news'*

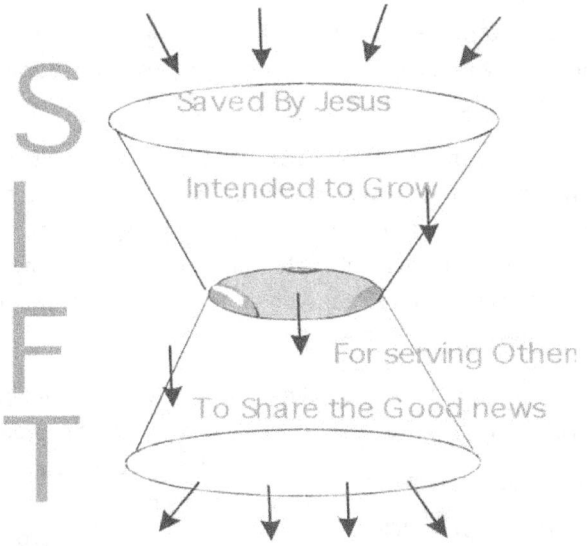

The concept of the *SIFT principle* is that it is bigger at the top and down the bottom than it is in the middle. It is part of the sifting process for everything to come into the top from many different areas and then as it goes through the sifting process it is refined. When it comes out the other end it has the potential to go everywhere again, but this time in better form than it began. So, can the process of growth be the same for us?

The idea of the *SIFT principle* is that you need as many entry points as possible for the kids to hear about Jesus. There is then a process by which they can grow and serve and understand the calling that God gives all of us to share the good news. Ensuring this process is known to all makes it possible for it to happen deliberately. It is not just a 'hope and see' kind of ministry.

The SIFTing process is an ongoing process. You are open to learning something, you grow in it and then share it with others. But it can be cyclic as well, we should be always open to saying 'yes' to Jesus, always growing, always serving and always sharing what we have learnt. This needs to happen over and over again, in our journey with Jesus.

When you program, plan and dream for your ministry, it is valuable to make sure that you have provided for every one of the four aspects of the SIFTing process.

This was useful for me and my team. We began to make sure that we had key ministries/programs/opportunities in each of the four steps which helped our children along the way. It kept us on track and helped us continually evaluate what we were doing, why we were doing it and where we were spending our energy and resources, which are often limited.

> **Each child's journey with God is an ongoing – or should I say 'on-growing' – process, and we are partly responsible for their progress on this journey**

The idea of the SIFT principle is that everyone is at one or another point of this process. Each child's journey with God is an ongoing – or should I say 'on-growing' – process, and we are partly responsible for their progress on this journey. We also need to emphasise the importance of the parent's role in this process, since they are the most powerful influence in a child's life at this stage.

Let me provide some practical examples that might work for you and your ministry.

STEP 1: SAVED BY JESUS

It is important to be always seeking ways to reach into the community and open up opportunities to connect with families and children who have not heard the Gospel message. It is also crucial to constantly challenge and immerse the kids you are ministering to in the message of Salvation as well.

Although there are many and varied ways to do this, there is no one set way. It will depend on your community's actual needs, as well as the resources you have in your teams of people. Here are simply a number of ways of connecting with those who do not know Jesus yet that I have seen work very well.

- **Religious Education in Schools**
  We have teachers in the local schools teaching SRE (Special Religious Education – or what we call 'Scripture'). This not only provides the opportunity to talk to not-yet Christians about Jesus, but also to make connections with them as ambassadors of Jesus. There are often many opportunities to advertise and share about other events and programs that we are involved in. Your relationship with the kids leads to them coming to other programs and events.

- **Recovery Courses**
  'Recovery' courses are for children and their families. They can be a great outreach and a wonderful ministry in their own right. They fulfill a need in the community as rates of family breakdown are high and children are not coping with the general stresses of life. These courses provide a chance for participants to talk about what is going on, to build a relationship with someone who becomes like a 'coach' to them. Recovery courses give them life skills for everyday situations and teach them about a God who is always with them, no matter what they go through. Courses like these have been a wonderful connection to not-yet Christian families, and great entry points to the faith. If you are interested in finding out more about such courses go to www.careforce.org.

- **Celebration Events/ Productions**
  Easter and Christmas can be great times to have wonderful family events. I know that at *Careforce Ministries* in Melbourne, Australia, one of their key outreach events happens the week before Christmas. They put on a massive, professional Christmas production and thousands of people in the community come to

it. People have learnt that it is an event you don't want to miss. They always have a strong Christian message throughout the production. It is a great entry point for many people. You need to determine where the strength in your church community lies, and see if God can use that to become an entry point. The Christian community I am now a part of is very strong in the creative arts. Our dream is to be able to present professional, family-based productions that might send a powerful message to the community. It is a dream we have, and we are running with it.

- **Playgroups**
Playgroups are a place where mothers (and some fathers) and their preschool-aged children can spend time together with their peers. Many playgroups are filled with not-yet Christians. You can have key mothers and workers there for the specific purpose of building relationships and to be a listening ear. They are a great connection with the community.

- **Specialised Camps**
We hold specialized camps for abused children and work with government departments such as DOCS, and specialist organizations like Barnardos. This has given us credibility with the government systems and also provided future links for these families. We take these kids away for a week of wonderful memories and unconditional love, and we teach them about Jesus. You can go to the website www.sckc.org.au to see more about these wonderful camps that truly change lives and are an entry point for these families to turn from their destructive pattern of life.

- **mainly Music**
mainly Music is a program designed for preschoolers and their parents to learn and play together while teaching their children something valuable about music. It is meeting a need for the kids and their parents in a positive environment. You can be

Jesus to them in the way you lead them.
See www.mainly-music.org

- **Adopt-a-Block**
I had the privilege of going to the Dream Centre in LA and was able to see the heartbeat of what they do as they reach out to their community. Of the many amazing ways they reach out and serve their community, I will endeavour to highlight just one. However, I'd encourage you to go their website www.dreamcenter.org and see what else they are doing to connect with their community.

Every Saturday, a group of people go out into the community and participate in what they call Adopt-a-Block. They simply spend the morning cleaning the area, fixing things in houses for free, playing with the kids on the street, providing breakfast for free and any other food supplies people might need. They are there to serve and have built up a trust and integrity amongst the community so that people cannot help but be drawn to this group of people and want to know why they are so different and loving.

- **Snack Attack**
This is a unique pastoral care system that lets children know that someone cares about them. If a child on the roll is away for more than three weeks they can be 'Snack Attacked'. This means that two people arrive on their front door one afternoon and when the door is opened, the visitors say "Snack Attack!". The child receives a bag with the following contents in it: a snack, a colouring-in competition or puzzle, information about what is coming up and anything you might want to add to that. It is short and sweet and easy to do, but makes a lasting impact. You can have the leaders dress up in a funny costume; you can take a picture of the child's response and give it to them; you can post the photo on a board (with their permission) so everyone knows who has been 'snack attacked' this week... It is also an incentive for the child to come

and see their picture and laugh with their friends about what happened. This is one simple way to show kids we care.

Children's Pastor Bill Wilson, working in New York City, USA, had someone visit every child in their Sidewalk Sunday School each week. They would only be at each child's house for 10 minutes, but he really believed that it was one of the main reasons why children kept coming back for more.

STEP 2: INTENDED TO GROW

We need to focus on actively helping our kids to grow in their relationship with Jesus. If there is nowhere they are being fed, we can be seen simply as a glorified babysitting service.

- **Sunday Ministries**

  Sunday ministries can be designed to provide a balanced experience of worship, service, learning and fellowship. Basically, we need to teach them 'churchmanship'. This can be done in a way that is exciting and relevant to their needs. Our kids loved to come to J-Zone and Veggie-Patch (a Sunday Ministry Program I was overseeing), but they also need to be growing in their faith as well.

- **Friendzy:**

  This was an after-school program. Once again, this was meeting a need in the community for care after school. However, the main aspect of this activity was that it was a 'friendly' atmosphere where kids got to hang out together, eat together and learn about Jesus. Many kids naturally brought their friends because they loved being there so much; they couldn't help but invite them!

  The difference with this program was that it was unashamed about its purpose – growing in God. So there was a limit to who would come. It was not just fun, games and entertainment. The kids who came knew that they were coming to learn and grow closer to Jesus. They did this in the form of a 40 minute small group study, with a leader and about 6– 10 kids in each group. The groups stayed the same and were split into age groups to help the group's dynamics.

- **Camps**

    There are many great reasons for camps, and 'intensive discipleship' is certainly one of them. A camping experience is so much more than getting away from the rat race. It is a place where you can break down barriers and misconceptions of the church. It is often a new setting, which allows you to do things differently. It is always an atmosphere where time is not your enemy and where you have time to BE together and to share so many new experiences.

    Camps are great for discipleship because it is a chance to see God work 24/7. I tell my leaders that the most challenging thing about being a leader at a camp is that you don't clock off.

    > *I tell my leaders that the most challenging thing about being a leader at a camp is that you don't clock off*

    As a leader in a cabin, the children see you at your best and worst times. It is at bedtime, when you are all lying in your beds and someone makes a smell that gases everyone out, and you are all laughing and blaming each other, that relationships can really begin. It is at those times that kids say the most amazing things.

    It is the time when you've been walking through the bush for an hour and you are all tired and thirsty that the question comes, "Where was God when I was being beaten up by my step-dad?" It is then that discipling happens – unplanned and out of context, right then and there where a child needs help and guidance and feels safe enough to ask the hard questions. These are the times when they need to see how God works in their lives, meeting their needs, and how He can heal their hurts.

The camp setting allows time for the children to see adults model Christ-centred living 24 hours a day. It's a great opportunity for modelling to kids, but it is especially valuable because being away for three days or even a week allows you to disciple with a 'complete' approach. You can teach and model in a well-rounded way. I mean by this that you are able to teach the children by meeting all their needs – physically, intellectually, socially and spiritually. You have the time to run a program that can connect with these needs and develop a very different discipleship program.

For example, a camp that I ran with the theme of 'MI Kidz' (standing for 'Mission Impossible Kids' or 'MY Kids' as in 'God's Kids') began with the gospel message and then took them on a journey to discover what it means to live with Christ. The learning came from interactive teaching, drama, music, comedy and ministry time. It also continued in small group projects where they had to perform physical tasks.

The time you have in a camp setting allows time for reflection, continued discussion and bouncing off other kids and leaders in the organized time as well as the down, unstructured time. It allows children to get involved and solve tasks and try new things they have never done before. Of course, this is all with food and sleep thrown in to keep the energies up.

At the end of the week they graduated as an MI Kid. They received a temporary tattoo to mark the occasion. They had to enter HQ (Head Quarters) which was set up in a loft of a small room. They had to climb up a ladder and enter their own unique code to see if they graduated. As they entered their code, the computer spoke back to them, "Welcome Sam Groves, you are now an MI Kid." Everything was shiny and fluorescent, and as they climbed down the ladder they were blindfolded. They were then taken to a secret room where the received their tattoo. It was a fantastic end to an amazing week. We built the anticipation all week, and the children left with many resources and keys to continue their relationship with God.

You can go to www.discoverylearningseries.com to find out more about great resources you can use for camps.

- **Courses**
  You can have short-term courses on any topic for kids. They can be 2– 6 weeks long. Kids sign up for them and they can even receive a certificate for doing them. We all love recognition and achievement. If Girl Guides and Boy Scouts can do this, why can't we? Make the topics relevant to them and their current situations, for example, 'Making good choices when watching TV', 'Hanging Tough with God at School' etc.

- **Life Groups**
  These can be small accountability and caring groups with 4– 5 kids and an adult. It can be formal/informal, structured/unstructured. You can meet monthly, weekly, or whatever you decide as a group. You can mix social time with prayer and sharing. Our kids need to feel like they belong. They need to feel they have someone to talk to, and they need to understand, hear and experience that God cares about their everyday lives.

  > **Our kids need to feel like they belong. They need to feel they have someone to talk to**

- **Twisted**
  This is a 'mentoring' system that aims at connecting an adult, a child and God together. Just as a three-stranded cord is not easily

broken (Ecclesiastes 4:12), so children will be more resilient to life's difficulties if they have a significant other in their life – apart from their parents – to whom they can talk about anything.

- **Parent's Support Resources**
Giving parents information to take home provides them with the tools to share with their kids about what they have been learning. You might be able to provide a library of great books and videos which the kids can take home and watch while they are with their parents. You might provide courses for parents that encourage them about how to help their kids grow spiritually.

The preschool my daughter attended often handed me resources and information sheets about how my child was developing and tips for helping them along. Surely children's workers can do this as well. After all, eternity is more important for the child than eating the right foods at preschool.

If there is a focus on supporting the parents rather than just running programs for their kids, you will be surprised how much you will empower the parents to take this responsibility upon themselves. Most don't do it because they feel inadequately equipped. You can help to change that.

STEP 3: FOR SERVING OTHERS

Ephesians 4:12-13(NIV) says that God gives gifts "to prepare (His) people for works of service, so that the body of Christ may be built up until we reach unity in the faith and in the knowledge of the Son of God and become mature, attaining to the whole measure of the fullness of Christ". What a powerful verse! It shows us that God calls us to serve so that we might grow and become mature. Pure discipleship has to be serving. It also talks of how serving builds the body and brings unity between the parts of the body. How awesome to be a part of something unified! This is what keeps most Christians strong in the faith, and in the same way, children will stay strong in the Lord when they are serving Him and using their gifts to serve the body.

There are many ways to ensure this happens with kids. There are endless possibilities, limited only by the unique features of your community and the areas in which your leaders and kids are gifted. Dream together of ways in which you can begin to serve.

> **Pure discipleship has to be serving**

Here are some examples of ways for kids to serve, based on the available leadership and the gifts of the kids that we were working with at the time:

- **Kids Choir**
  A choir can minister to adults in very powerful ways. They can sing wherever they are invited. You can pray with them regularly and teach them about what it means to minister in song and not just perform.

- **Dance Troupe**
  A dance troupe can work on dances for the purposes of expressing a message, and they also can minister wherever the opportunities arise.

- **KIA (Kids in Action)**
  We established this group for children aged 11– 12 years. They were trained and encouraged to find ways in which they could serve others. They were given a special badge and had extra responsibilities in whatever programs were deemed appropriate. They could serve with the younger children. They could help in areas such as buddying up with a younger child, serving the morning tea, helping on registration, etc.

- **Junior Leadership**
  The teenage years are when kids are really struggling with fitting in, so we began a Junior Leadership Program. They received a

badge and a T-shirt. They started to help lead in worship, drama, technical processes, leading games, leading small groups and did whatever they wanted to try in order to discover their gifts from God. They had training events throughout the year. I believe it was a key to not losing them to the world.

STEP 4: TO SHARE THE GOOD NEWS

Of course, we are not taking discipleship seriously until we understand that we are called to share the Good News with others. For a long time we have felt that children are too young (some still believe that). However, this is an important aspect of discipleship as it puts all they have learnt and discovered into action and shows them that Christ actually has something for them to do in this life.

- **Mission Trips**
  Children should have opportunities to be involved in small local outreaches throughout the year with other churches, in hospitals, or helping out in the community in whatever way is appropriate in your area.

> **'to be involved in mission' is to sacrifice and be other-people-centred**

  They should be given the opportunity to go on a mission trip where they present the Gospel to kids in another country. I believe that by giving kids this opportunity at the end of their time in children's ministry, you send them out with a great experience and the right perspective – a real understanding that Christ wants to use them in a mighty way. They should be encouraged to raise their own money, because 'to be involved in mission' is to sacrifice and be other-people-centred. They experience another culture, they are thankful for what they have, and experience the fact that they can give something they have to others. It can be as simple as giving a toothbrush and toiletries, to as complex as helping other children learn the English language.

CHAPTER 8 - THE VITAL EDGES - 4: DISCIPLESHIP

There are many ways to see this process of discipleship develop. It is a matter of simply having a deliberate process in place. I have given you some ideas that I have seen work successfully over the years.

I have seen these ideas work successfully over the years, but please do not be limited by them. I know God will have bigger and better ideas for you that will be specific to your community, resources and gifts. Work through the questions at the end of this chapter to begin dreaming God's dreams for you and your ministry.

IMPORTANT ASPECTS OF DISCIPLING CHILDREN

- **Time in relationship**
  We seriously underestimate the time we spend 'hanging' with kids. If you think about the best times that you have had with your own friends, they would probably be times that are unplanned, or have come out of just being together.

> **We seriously underestimate the time we spend 'hanging' with kids**

In my family, mealtimes have always been special times. We get together at Mum and Dad's house. There is my brother and sister-in-law, my husband and I, all our kids and Mum and Dad. Mum puts on a great meal and we are all still at the table at 11.30pm talking and laughing and sharing. There are no plans apart from simply being together and eating. Don't underestimate the power of a meal. I am convinced that these can be the most special times. Relationships are best built when time is not an issue and there is space for anything to happen. When we began the KIA group (Kids in Action) at our church, I had ten kids over for a sleepover at my house along with two other adults. They were coming at 7pm for pizza and then leaving the next morning after breakfast. Being an organiser by nature, I thought, "Oh my gosh... What are we going to do with all this time?" So I arranged for a big screen to watch a movie, planned some games to play and had lots of food ready if they got bored.

At the time, my golden retriever had 5 puppies, which were 5 weeks old and very cute. I hid them away in a small room downstairs so they would be out of the way. When the kids got there they were very excited about seeing the puppies. We went down to the small room and virtually stayed there all night. We left the big room upstairs with the big screen movie and all the food and games, and spent most of the night cuddling puppies and just hanging and talking. By about 10pm I got all the kids and adults to come upstairs to have supper and talk. We talked about dreams and ways we want to serve others. We then had a prayer time that was awesome, and every kid prayed. They prayed deep, wonderful and inspiring prayers. It was a great time together.

We didn't get much sleep that night. We laughed, mucked around and had a fun breakfast. When it was finished they all left and I sat down and thought, "That was a great time! We didn't do much, but something happened overnight that was special amongst us all!" That year, I watched this group of kids develop a great bond that was special. They grew in their spirituality, particularly their 'other-centeredness'. They are still growing. It is hard to define what happened that night, but it was 'discipleship'.

- **Role modelling**
One of the most powerful ways to teach children is to model a way of life. For many of the children that we work with, just to be in the presence of people who live aiming to honor God is a real eye-opener for them. The world they come from is so different that I am amazed how obvious this is to them. This is not to say that we are perfect and that if they come into my home they will see a perfect Christian family, but when a child grows up in an

environment where God's values are not a priority, even the way we talk to each other can surprise them.

In this way, time spent in relationship, the way we play a game, how we handle things when they go wrong, how we cope when they misbehave, what boundaries we might enforce, all say something about what we value. We are role modelling all the time. Role modelling is most effective at camps and low-key programs where the children get to see the real you! The old adage "Things are more often caught than taught" says it all. Never underestimate what you are teaching children just by being in the room with them. I watch leaders say many things, but their actions say a whole lot more without them even realizing it.

> ***Things are more often caught than taught***

Consider what our actions can communicate about the real us:

- When a leader must be the centre of attention, and demonstrates this by calling out when someone else is leading, they could be modelling, "I need to be the focus, because I like all the attention. It makes me feel important."
- When a leader must have children all around them, they could be modelling, "I need you to like me, because I lack confidence to think I am lovable without your attention."
- When a leader interrupts and makes jokes all the time while someone else is leading, they could be modelling, "I want people to think that I am funny, because that is what makes me feel valuable."
- When a leader will not let a child win at a game, they could be modelling, "My pride needs to be fed, so I cannot let you see me fail at something."
- When a leader will not be involved in something messy and dirty, or isn't prepared to dress up for fun, they could be modelling, "I must always look respectable in public; it is important to me how I look."

It is always a good idea to check our motivation; why do we do things and what are we communicating when we behave that way? Whether we like it or not, we are mainly teaching children by what we DO.

- **Allowing kids to choose**

    We do a lot of teaching with kids and it is often classed by them as being 'boring and irrelevant'. One of the solutions is to have the children choose to do it themselves. It changes the whole atmosphere. One of the most difficult aspects of Sunday ministry is that often our children are not there by personal choice. We all know what happens when we are forced to do something we don't want to do, even if it is exciting.

    When I was 15, I was forced to go on a holiday to Europe. What an awesome opportunity and experience. We travelled through 8 countries in 3 weeks and saw the most amazing sites. Yet as I read through my diaries of that trip, they confirm my personal memories that I was absolutely miserable. All I wanted to do was be home with my friends and boyfriend! Sometimes, it doesn't matter how wonderful the experience is, if the kids don't have a choice. They tend to dig their heels in and are determined not to have a good time, no matter how awesome the experience is.

    We began a program mid-week, which the kids could choose to come to. We did things there that, if we did them on a Sunday, the kids would never put up with. We were unashamed that we were there to learn about Jesus and to grow in Him. Of the 2 hours, 40 minutes was spent in small groups studying the Bible. If it's the kids' choice to come, it makes all the difference with what you can do with them.

- **Teaching applied to daily life**

    It is important to understand that we don't tend to learn anything unless we can see the need for it in our lives. When we teach anything, it is our job to make sure that it is actually something that is helpful for daily living. This is a key principal for teaching, and is especially important to discipleship. If we were truly doing that well, children would not be walking away at the age of 11–12 saying that Jesus has no relevance to their lives.

At *Friendzy* (the after-school discipleship club), we aimed to challenge the kids to put into action what they were learning. Each week, we honoured kids who applied what they had learnt to their everyday living. On one occasion, after we had been challenging the kids about finding their part in the body of Christ, a girl called Charlotte came up to me with a poem that she had written during the week. I read it out to the whole group, and we celebrated the great thought that had gone into writing such a poem. It was wonderful to see her putting what she had learnt into some sort of action.

> **When we teach anything, it is our job to make sure that it is actually something that is helpful for daily living**

You are not always going to receive feedback about the effectiveness of what you are doing. Evaluation, in this respect, is hard. It has to be seen as a long-term thing. Each year, you should be able to see the growth in the children you are ministering to – to see real change. This is the best form of evaluation.

TAKE SOME TIME TO REFLECT:

1. Think about your growth in God? When has this been effective? Who helped in that process and how did they help?

_____
_____
_____
_____
_____
_____
_____

2. Spend some time thinking about what you believe about the process of discipleship for a person's life.

_____
_____
_____
_____
_____
_____
_____

3. Take 1/2 a day working through what a strategy might be for you and your team and begin to put a pathway of purpose in place where you minister.

_____
_____
_____
_____
_____
_____
_____

CHAPTER 9

The connecting pieces
Connecting pieces, like the icing on a cake, ensures the picture shines through clearly

The middle pieces are important and necessary for finishing the puzzle. They are like the icing or the filling that makes a cake taste extra good. Although without them you still have a framework so you know what the puzzle is about, the middle pieces are important because they help connect and finish the puzzle.

I have spent the last 15 years training others and speaking on these middle piece topics. However, they are only important when they are used within the context of the edges and corner pieces – that is, once you have set the right edges in place for your ministry. My concern is that I have seen so many programs, children's ministries, curricula and even children's pastors who do these connecting pieces well, while still missing the heart of what they are about.

It is possible to be able to use these connecting pieces well with kids and yet never lead a child to Christ, never help children grow closer to God and only give the kids a 'good time'. We must be about more than entertaining kids and offering them fun experiences. While I want to be on the cutting edge with the way in which I connect to kids, it is worth nothing if they

> **We must be about more than entertaining kids and offering them fun experiences**

walk away at 12 years of age thinking I was a cool teacher but they don't know Jesus. This is my greatest fear in children's ministry. All the 'whiz bang' methods in the world do not replace the message of Christ and an active relationship with Him.

I began this book by telling you about a puzzle that I did with my son, Sam. I remember it was a picture of the Great Barrier Reef, a beautiful paradise under the north east waters off the Australian Sunshine Coast. It is filled with beautifully coloured fish and gorgeous coral.

We got to the point in the puzzle where we had all the vital edges in place. The sense of excitement was growing because we could see that the picture was going to be beautiful. If we'd stopped there we would have had an idea what it was about, and it certainly looked pretty. We looked around the edges and saw bits of fish - we could imagine how pretty they would look; but the connecting pieces would bring clarity to the whole picture and reveal the parts we couldn't fill in with our imagination

ANTICIPATION AND EXCITEMENT ABOUT LEARNING

Setting the framework for kids entices them – they are filed with anticipation and excitement – and then the scene is set for real learning. Once children are excited and full of anticipation for what the picture is about, the connecting pieces help 'cement' the message for the kids.

Although the Barrier Reef puzzle was hard for Sam, he wanted to continue so he could see how beautiful the completed picture was going to be. The edges and corners (the framework) helped him. He was captured, drawn in, and he became open to learning anything at that point. Remember, as we fl esh out these connecting pieces, never place the importance of these elements higher than the framework.

MAKING IT REAL

Here are some thoughts on making it real in order to truly connect with this generation:

- Stop teaching at them and start empowering them to begin discovering for themselves the difference Jesus can actually make in their life.
- Stop speaking at them and start putting them into situations that allow them to experience that God's truth is real.
- Stop forcing them to listen to you and allow them instead to interact in the experience so that they can be a part of the learning process.
- Stop telling them stories of other people's lives that have been changed by God and start challenging them about their own lives.
- Stop using just the spoken word and explore the many ways to communicate that can be much more powerful than the spoken word.
- Stop making them sit and watch you and encourage them to start serving and doing ministry for themselves.
- Stop calling Sunday ministry "Sunday School" – which reinforces that it should only be done on Sundays and that it should be something like school.
- Stop expounding God's word without first meeting the needs of our generation and addressing them where they are at.

It is *experiences,* within relationships, that kids never forget. Few of us would still be in Christian ministry today if we hadn't experienced Jesus in a transforming, real way in our own lives. Yet so often we ask our children to settle for our stories or the stories of distant characters from the Bible, and just trust that if it happened to them it must be real.

Walt Disney Pictures produced a film called *The Pacifier*[56] starring Vin Diesel. It was a great family movie but as is the case with so many Disney movies, there were also many great things to learn from it. Here we have this highly trained navy seal, capable and passionate about his work, on a mission to save a family. He approaches this mission like any other. He is the boss, he knows what is best, and goes about laying down a plan that he knows will keep this family safe from

---
[56] *The Pacifier,* Walt Disney Pictures, 2005

harm. The trouble is that he is working with a group of kids who say to him, "We are not listening to you until you prove to us that this is going to actually help us." He tries to put systems into place to help them stay safe, but they just ignore or block him out anyway they can.

> **Getting real is the way we will connect with this generation**

We might be passionate and know the truth. We may even be highly qualified to teach these kids about Jesus. But they are simply saying, "Get real." No matter what the Pacifier does or says, the kids will not take him seriously until their house is broken into and he literally saves their lives. NOW they are willing. That might seem extreme to you, but for our kids, in this extreme world, who are desensitised to what they really need, it takes something serious to happen for them to really listen. (I am not just talking about kids here either. Adults today can be even harder to reach...) But let's make kids our focus: Getting real is the way we will connect with this generation.

As the movie progresses, we see that the Pacifier now has the children's attention and they are willing to listen to him. He also begins to learn himself, and by spending time with them, begins to take his truth and mould it individually to each child based upon their needs and likes, but mainly their life issues. He begins to help the young girl gain confidence in who she is through her 'fire flies' activities. He begins to help the older boy discover who he is through his acting, and so on. Through relationship, by starting where they are at, he applies what he wants to teach them. He grows from saying, "I don't do cookie selling" or "drama directing" to becoming the best 'den mother' and a fantastic director.

I can hear you saying, "Hold on, Tammy, this is Hollywood!" That may be true, but didn't Paul say in 1 Corinthians 9: 22, (NIV) "I have become all things to all men in order that I might save some"? My personal experience is the same. In order to connect with kids I have tried a good many things through relationship and getting involved

CHAPTER 9 - THE CONNECTING PIECES

with their likes and dislikes and their life issues (all for the purpose of teaching truth). *The Pacifier* demonstrates well that the key to connecting is having that kind of breakthrough experience with kids; only then will they see how 'real' you are.

It is hard to plan or precisely define when this moment happens, but you know when it does. Group Publishing (a renowned publisher of Christian educational resources) would call it the 'a-ha' moment. This has become a common term amongst Christian Children's workers. I have found ministry is all about working on how to create these moments which create a platform for God to do what He wants to. These become the connecting pieces for growing closer to God.

In the next chapters we will look at four ways we can work with this generation of kids in order to create that moment where connection takes place. From that point, anything can happen! Lives change and we see God do amazing things.

 **TAKE SOME TIME TO REFLECT ON THE FOLLOWING QUESTIONS:**

1. Go back to pages 130-131 and look at the 'Stops'. Which ones do you know you have been guilty of? How can you bring about change in these areas?

   _____
   _____
   _____
   _____
   _____

2. Under the word 'START' below, rewrite the 'Stop' sentences on pages 130-131 using the opposite action that would be more positive to help connect with kids today.
   START:

   _____
   _____
   _____
   _____
   _____
   _____

3. Think about a 'get real' moment in your life that connected with you in such a way that it changed something significant in your life. Take some time to write about it and think about what was happening for you at the time. What principles can you take from your own experiences and implement into your teaching of kids?

   _____
   _____
   _____
   _____
   _____
   _____

CHAPTER 10

The connecting pieces
1: ACTIVATING

To activate someone is to get them to actively take a part in the learning process

To activate someone is to make them an active part of what is happening. Even the static entertainment world has seen the value of this form of communication. Many popular TV shows speak to children as if they are right in the TV with them.

I remember observing my daughter when she was two years old, watching *Bear in the Big Blue House*. Bear (the main character) came closer to the screen and asked her what she had been doing because she smelled like flowers. She had no problem responding, "No bear, I don't smell like flowers" and giggled as she walked away from the front of the screen. She was totally in the moment and reacting to him even though he was on TV.

This activating process is very effective and is the reason our highest rating TV shows and games are all based on the audience being actively involved. This may be through being able to vote someone on or off a team, or by being able to connect to the game so that it responds to you, for example, through controllers or Eye Toy cameras. You no longer see people just sitting in front of games with controllers when you walk past a video game arcade. Now they are on jet skis, dance pads, snow skis and motorbikes. It is all based on being active in the process.

The sad reality of this is that it is often replacing the real active experiences that kids and adults are able to have. There was a time where people would get together and play basketball. Now they stand in a room on their own and play against someone in another country. There was a time when people would have table tennis tournaments together. Just recently I was walking in a mall where a guy with an imaginary paddle was bouncing a ball at a screen with an imaginary person on the screen bouncing it back at him.

> *A wonderful gift we can offer to our children is to give them real-life active experiences with real people and real situations*

The sad reality of being a champion basketball player on a PS2 is that it gives you no skills for real life and it teaches you nothing about other people and working with them. It doesn't teach you how to persevere when you can't get a slam dunk or how you handle losing to another person. You can't just press 'start again' and erase the score as if it never happened. A wonderful gift we can offer to our children is to give them real-life active experiences with real people and real situations. This brings about real consequences and real learning opportunities.

One camp that I ran was called 'Actual Reality'. It was based on challenging kids in actual (as opposed to virtual) active situations where they learned by interacting with each other. At this camp we put the kids through a week's worth of challenging activities and situations where they had to learn to work together, communicate, handle conflict and work with their own weaknesses.

So much of our teaching has always been in the traditional way where students sit and listen to the 'expert' teach at them. To promote activity means the teacher must become the 'fellow enquirer' and

CHAPTER 10 - THE CONNECTING PIECES - 1: ACTIVATING

coach, and the kids become the active learners. We need to go with what happens in group experiences and see what they come up with themselves. Sometimes it is not exactly what we had planned, but it is always worthwhile, for it is learning from the perspective of the children's own interests. In an active simulation game, a question that comes from a child is a powerful moment of learning, because the child wants to know something and is therefore more open to take it on board.

This style of teaching is powerful when it comes to connecting with kids. Therefore, when we want to teach a child something the question to ask ourselves is, "How can I get them actively involved in this learning experience?" This is the question I ask whenever I am writing and working out how I want to teach something to a group of people. It has completely changed the way I teach. My teaching has become more about setting a situation up and being willing to journey with kids during the learning process, rather than me working hard on a story and having them captivated by my story telling.

On a personal level this was very releasing for me, as I would often watch great puppeteers, ventriloquists, magicians, and dramatic storytellers and think, "I just can't do that, so how can I work with children?" For all of you who feel that way, I am here to tell you that there are other ways that in the long run can be even more powerful and have a longer lasting effect on the children's lives.

If you think back to a powerful time in your life that had a profound effect on you, I can almost guarantee that you would have had an active involvement in the process. Even to ask Jesus into your heart has to be something that you actively do yourself. No one can force you or do it for you. The best storyteller in the world may challenge you, but in the end it must be something you act upon or it is not real for you.

This is why I believe worship can be such a powerful active experience. Children's Ministries Specialist, Phil Schroeder, says about his work with children in worship, "I usually provide a plank for us to walk off and let the sea do the rest".[57]

> **Phil Schroeder: I usually provide a plank for us to walk off and let the sea do the rest**

So, if you want to challenge kids about serving God, get them to actually do it. If you want to challenge them about leadership, get them to begin serving and taking on a leadership role. If you want to challenge them about trusting God, find ways to help them actively understand how to trust God in everyday things. If you want them to learn about self-sacrifice, get them doing things that require self-sacrifice. It will be so much more powerful than simply talking about it, or talking about your experiences.

In the end, if they don't actively see how it works for their life, they will walk away believing that it is fine for you but it is not for them. This is simply what is happening right now. Our children are walking away from God saying He is not relevant, even when they know John 3:16 and the stories of the Old Testament.

Some of the most rewarding times in ministry are empowering kids to be active and watching them grow and develop in God. I believe ministry is more about getting others involved than for me to be the one ministering to the kids from the front. My focus over the past five or six years has gradually become more about developing leaders, and developing opportunities for children and families to be activated in their own learning.

For years I have spoken at conferences to hundreds of people feeling like this was the best use of my time and gifts for God. Yet over the past few years I have come to realize that if I am to follow Jesus' example, I will be spending significant times with a few people and helping them to be transformed by God. Even at the most challenging conferences, it is really up to the person to go home and actually do

---

[57] L Sweet, *"SoutTsunami,"* Zondervan Publishing House, Grand Rapids, Michigan, 1999, p. 220

something with what they have learnt, because unless they do they will never change.

During the past five years we have been trying to do something different. I run a conference called '@ctiv@te' where a maximum of 25 people come from all over Australia. They come to be actively involved in the learning experience. The conference is run alongside a children's camp, so the delegates begin by watching how we communicate and work with the children. They then have some input and teaching. Then it is time for them to put that into action by actively doing it there and then with a group of kids in a controlled environment where there are leaders to support them and give them constructive feedback. The feedback from this conference confirms that the participants actually go away from the active experience changed, and that the children's ministries they go back to are never the same because *they* are not the same.

There is a similar result when you do this for kids. If kids in your ministry actually experience God and see how He can make a difference in their lives, they will grow and change and become more like Jesus. You must see the 'active' process as the glue which helps the lessons stick.

> **You must see the 'active' process as the glue which helps the lessons stick**

This means that if you leave your ministries or move churches, or if the kids and families move and change, their active experience with Jesus will never leave them. It is in them because it has happened to them. That's what Jesus did to the twelve with whom He spent three years. When he left, they carried on with the ministry. I want to empower kids in this way, to be responsible for leading them closer to Jesus and then let Him take them where He wants to.

When we involve kids in experiences, we need to start with their interests. A teaching concept we worked through with kids which was very effective was when we took the interest that our kids had with collecting cards *(Yu-Gi-Oh!* and *Pokemon,* etc) and used it as the basis for teaching them about the vital things that they need to live life well. They collected cards based on what we were teaching them. Then we put them into a life-sized maze where the kids had to put into action what they had been learning. They had to get through the maze and through challenges that required them using the knowledge they had already gained. This was such a powerful example of the point I have made about active experiences helping lessons stick like glue. They couldn't wait to go into the maze, and they couldn't wait to collect their cards. They were totally involved in the process, they loved it, and along the way they were learning.

The Xtreme Games are a very popular sporting event in Australia. Wherever you turn, sportspeople are trying to do things that have never been done before. There's an element of danger in all that they do. The director of the Planet X games said, "It's the whole Evel Knievel thing. Everybody knows there's a chance of seeing a good crash. The whole 'don't-try-this-at-home' thing draws the crowds".[58]

This generation is busting to do something daring and exciting – something that pushes the boundaries; and we wonder why they find church boring? In all honesty, I love God, but I can often find church boring! What I don't find boring, though, is serving Him, living for Him and being with Him. There is nothing more exciting than seeing kids grasp hold of the concept of living for Jesus and starting to serve and grow in their relationship with Him. What are we doing as children's workers to fuel this quest?

I know that the encouragement and opportunity I was given to sing on stage from the age of 8 in the church my family attended was a key for me staying strong with God. When you are serving, you are not only doing (experiencing) something, you are also forced to grow and rely on God as you step out and try something new. I saw this with the children who came up through KIA (Kids in Action as described in Chapter 8) and began serving. Since they did not want to stop when they were too old to be part of the children's ministry,

---

[58] *"Who" Magazine Article:* "X marks the Spot" Written by Jennie Noonan, November Issue, 2001.

CHAPTER 10 - THE CONNECTING PIECES - 1: ACTIVATING

we began a Junior Leadership Program. At an age when most kids are dropping out and trying new things in their teenage years, these kids were growing and thriving as Christians and serving with more commitment than some of my best leaders. Yes, they needed supervision, guidance, and encouragement; yes, they stepped over the line sometimes, messed up and said the wrong thing. But they were learning and growing. Not one of them has cut someone's ear off in anger yet, so we're doing OK.

I had children busting to be in a KIA program. I had a Junior Leader ask me when she would be too old to be Junior Leader. When I asked why, she said, "Because I love it so much, I am not looking forward to not being able to do it." I informed her that she would never be too old to lead others as long as she stayed close to God.

Our kids are looking for something they can do while living on this earth that might make a difference. The amount of reality TV around just shows how desperately everyone wants those 30 seconds of fame. I took my son and his friend to see the movie Spy Kids, which we all loved. As we were taking his friend home, I overheard them talking about the movie. Sam said, "Wouldn't it be awesome if we were spies and could really save the world?" As they were both dreaming and talking about it, it set me thinking...We ARE a part of a mission to save the world! That is Jesus' mission and He chooses us to share in that. He chooses to use whoever is willing to speak out for the cause. From that thought emerged the 10-week program called MI Kidz (explained previously in Chapter 8) where we put kids into training to find their place in the mission and to help God save the world.

> **Our kids are looking for something they can do while living on this earth that might make a difference**

Many 11– 14 years old boys in Australia today are choosing to end their life for lack of any reason for living. There is no cause, no purpose, no reason that they can see worth living for. We have to do something about changing these facts. God has the answer. God has a purpose for them. There is a reason to live and a chance to live forever. The Bible is very clear that we are born with a purpose that is unique to us (Jeremiah 29:11). The exciting quest in life is to find what our purpose is in Christ and live it to the end.

Another time we picked up on the Xtreme Games concept and challenged kids to go 'Over the Edge' for Him. We have dropped them into 'Xtreme' challenges where they must put what they have learnt into action. We have put them through life-sized mazes, kidnapped them on buses, taken over meetings, and thrown children into many simulation experiences to help them see that serving God is not boring. In fact, it is a challenge that only the strong will survive.

Making the point with your kids can be achieved through an extravagant experience like in a camp setting, a simulation game, or something as simple as a 10 minute exercise. I remember a time when I had to teach kids in an RE class about God having authority over blindness. I took the class outside in pairs, with one child from each pair wearing a blindfold. While the blindfolded child walked around outside, I made sure that the other child was close by so they didn't hurt themselves. I asked them to do it in silence, as that gave them more of an experience of being lost and helpless. The children enjoyed the experience and were totally engaged.

I then asked them to sit down right where they were, and with their blindfolds still on, I asked them to tell me what they felt when they were actively experiencing the feeling of being blind. I asked them to keep their blindfolds on while they sat and listened to my story. They listened intently as I spoke to them about the man born blind and what Jesus did for him. One girl raised her hand and asked, "If Jesus was here, and someone was blind, could he make them see?" I said, "Yes, he has that authority. The question is, would you believe it if your saw it?" She said "Yes".

At that exact moment, the bell rang, and the kids went, "Ohh...", for they were so disappointed that the time had ended. I said, "Well, that is interesting. You'll all have to stay tuned till next week to see what happened to the people who saw this man suddenly able to see!" We finished our time together and the kids were keen the next week to see how it all ended.

Simple but engaging fun, and yet they were learning the whole time. Are you willing to ask the question, "How can I get them involved in the process?" You might be surprised where that question takes you.

 ## SOME PERSONAL CHALLENGES FOR THE WAY YOU ACTIVATE KIDS TODAY

1. When you look at your teaching style, does it allow kids to be actively involved or does it ask them to sit and listen?

   _____
   _____
   _____

2. Assess the time you spend with the kids you minister to. Is there scope for them to be involved in the learning process? Think of some practical ways to help the children get active! For example:

   - Areas of leadership
   - Supper/afternoon tea
   - Worship
   - Small group work
   - Bible reading
   - Registration
   - Drama
   - Technical
   - Buddying younger children
   - Games

   _____
   _____
   _____

3. Look over the next three weeks of teaching that you have ahead of you. Take some time in preparation and ask the question, "How can I get the children actively involved in the learning process?"

   _____
   _____
   _____
   _____

4. Spend some time at a local video game parlour or with the latest Xbox, Eye Toy or PlayStation game. Experience for yourself the way in which children are used to being involved in the process. Reflect on this experience and how it can help us change the way we approach the learning process with our kids.

   _____
   _____
   _____
   _____

The connecting pieces
2: EXPERIENTIAL
Our kids need to live experience, not just consume it

Our kids need to live experience, not just consume it. We all know that they are good consumers. They are after the next experience, then the next. They are never satisfied. Why is that? They are searching for something, but the next big thrill is not satisfying enough for them. If we are going to keep up with this kind of experiential living, we need to be helping others around us to know Christ in a real way (that is, to be 'missional').

It is the same for our kids. Our kids need to be 'in' the world, not just singing inside a church and always saying, "Come to us". They can minister in church, they can be growing in our churches, but unless they go out with the message, they will not be missional, nor will we be helping them to experience that being a Christian is an active, living, everyday thing. "The proof of people's faith is not in the information they know or the religious gatherings they

> *The proof of people's faith is not in the information they know or the religious gatherings they attend, but in the way they integrate what they know and believe into their everyday practices*

attend, but in the way they integrate what they know and believe into their everyday practices."[59]

BELIEVING OR EXPERIENCING: WHICH COMES FIRST?

Over the years, many adults have responded negatively to this issue. They struggle with kids doing ministry and serving before they totally understand all the theology, or before they have made a solid commitment to Christ. It is an interesting question; something like, "Which comes first, the chicken or the egg?"

Many would have a theology that says a child cannot truly understand the abstract concept of faith and grace, so they cannot be Christian until the teenage years. It follows that we can't sing worship songs with kids, because they can't worship a God they don't know. We can't have them leading, serving or teaching until they know Christ, and so on.

Leonard Sweet would say, "When our kids say 'Get real', they don't mean 'Prove it', or 'Give me the truth'. They mean 'Give me an experience, and then I'll see whether or not I will believe it.'"[60] In other words, unless we give them experiences, they will not believe Jesus and that He is real.

This statement had a profound effect on my life when I first read it. As educators, our purpose is for the truth to become real to children so that they might follow Jesus. But if what Leonard Sweet says is right, then all the head knowledge in the world will not make an ounce of difference unless they can first experience that Jesus' truth actually works in 'real' life. Unless it works for them, they will not believe it.

This fits with so many other aspects of our human nature that I have come to believe are true, such as the fact that we almost never learn from someone else's mistake. Most often we have to try it for ourselves, completely mess up and hopefully learn from the first time not to do it again. The main value in sharing your failures is not to

---

[59] George Barna, *Revolution: Finding Vibrant Faith Beyond the Walls of the Sanctuary*, Tyndale House Publishing, Illinois, USA, 2005, p. 25

[60] Leonard Sweet *SoulTsumani: Sink or Swim in New Millennium Culture*, Zondervan, Grand Rapids, 1999, p. 215

stop other people from making the same mistake, but merely to give them somewhere to come when they mess up too! Also, the times in life that have had the most impact on me are those occasions when I have personally experienced doing something rather than watching someone else.

In the movie *Chasing Liberty*,[61] Mandy Moore plays the US President's teenage daughter. She is someone who technically has the world at her fingertips, but she is never really allowed to experience any of it. She is always with a chaperone and is protected in everything she does. All she wants to do is to have her own experience, so she tries to run away while in Prague in order to begin her adventure through Europe. The President realizes that she needs to experience life for herself, but nevertheless arranges for someone to always be available to protect her if she needs it. She makes mistakes and gets herself into trouble many times, but even though she thinks she is on her own adventure, there is always someone there to help her.

In some ways, this is the role we are to play: setting up situations that are safe, yet allow for our kids to experience something for themselves, and learn from the good and bad. We become the fellow enquirer, and they have life changing experiences in the process.

In the book *Church, Next*, the authors explore the missional church today and how we are going to reach this next generation. They do not suggest that it is only 'experience' that is necessary for non-Christians to come to faith, but rather that for too long we have focused solely on 'head knowledge'. "Here we note that the barriers to faith were not intellectual as much as experiential and behavioural."[62]

> **Here we note that the barriers to faith were not intellectual as much as experiential and behavioural**

---

[61] *Chasing Liberty*, Warner Bros. Entertainment, 2004

[62] Eddie Gibbs & Ian Coffey, *Church Next: Quantum Changes in Christian Ministry*, 2001, p. 170

Let's look at what the Bible teaches us about this. In Luke 24, there is a story that is a wonderful example of which comes first – believing or experiencing.

> That same day two of them were walking to the village Emmaus, about seven miles out of Jerusalem. They were deep in conversation, going over all these things that had happened. In the middle of their talk and questions, Jesus came up and walked along with them. But they were not able to recognize who he was.
>
> He asked, "What's this you're discussing so intently as you walk along?"
>
> They just stood there, long-faced, like they had lost their best friend. Then one of them, his name was Cleopas, said, "Are you the only one in Jerusalem who hasn't heard what's happened during the last few days?" (Luke 24:13-18)[63]

Here are two of Jesus disciples. They were with Jesus when he died and they were devastated; they don't know what to believe now that Jesus is dead. Even when Jesus comes alongside of them and talks to them, they don't recognize Him. They were so caught up in their situation, confused and maybe even doubting all that they had seen.

> He said, "What has happened?"
>
> They said, "The things that happened to Jesus the Nazarene. He was a man of God, a prophet, dynamic in work and word, blessed by both God and all the people. Then our high priests and leaders betrayed him, got him sentenced to death, and crucified him. And we had our hopes up that he was the One, the One about to deliver Israel. And it is

---

[63] Eugene H Peterson, *The Message: The Bible in Contemporary Language,* NavPress Publishing Group, 2002

CHAPTER 11 - THE CONNECTING PIECES - 2: EXPERIENTIAL

> now the third day since it happened. But now some of our women have completely confused us.
>
> Early this morning they were at the tomb and couldn't find his body. They came back with the story that they had seen a vision of angels who said he was alive. Some of our friends went off to the tomb to check and found it empty just as the women said, but they didn't see Jesus." (Luke 24:19-24)[64]

Here they are sharing the Good News with Jesus Himself! They are admitting they are confused, and even though they have all the facts, the head knowledge, do they believe what has been happening? I would say no; at this stage they are questioning everything. Sometimes words and head knowledge are just not enough!

> Then he said to them, "So thick-headed! So slow-hearted! Why can't you simply believe all that the prophets said? Don't you see that these things had to happen, that the Messiah had to suffer and only then enter into His glory?" Then he started at the beginning, with the Books of Moses, and went on through all the Prophets, pointing out everything in the Scriptures that referred to him. (Luke 24:25-27)[65]

Jesus then even goes through all the Scriptures with them and yet they still doubt. Now for the key verse in this story.

> They came to the edge of the village where they were headed. He acted as if he was going on but they pressed him: "Stay and have supper with us. It's nearly evening; the day is done." So he went in with them. And here is what happened: He sat down at the table with them. Taking the

---

[64] Eugene H Peterson, *The Message: The Bible in Contemporary Language*, NavPress Publishing Group, 2002

[65] Eugene H Peterson, *The Message: The Bible in Contemporary Language*, NavPress Publishing Group, 2002

bread, he blessed and broke and gave it to them. At that moment, open-eyed, wide-eyed, they recognized him. And then he disappeared. (Luke 24:28-31)[66]

It was when Jesus broke the bread that they suddenly remembered their own experience, and it all came back to them in a flood, all that they had known in their heart about Him. The experience of breaking bread with Him in the upper room before He died was an experience they would never forget. It was an experience that they had not understood until they met Jesus again and THEN it all became clear.

"Rather than dismiss these experiences a priori, perhaps we should acknowledge that religious people of all times, of all ages, and, very likely, of all traditions have had mysterious encounters with the sacred that the rational mind, and more particularly, enlightenment science, simply cannot comprehend."[67]

So often we teach children by telling them what to believe and quoting from the Scriptures; but our children, like the disciples, are over on the other side of the track in their worlds of confusion and doubt. Our kids today are bombarded with choices, and fears of being bullied, failing at school, and families breaking down and separating. They are often screaming for help. They are saying, "Show me that Jesus really knows how I feel when I am in my room listening to my mum and dad screaming in the kitchen, and then I will be happy to learn more about Him. But don't just assume that because I'm in your Sunday school class, or a Religious Education Class, or at a camp in the school

---

[66] Eugene H Peterson, *The Message: The Bible in Contemporary Language,* NavPress Publishing Group, 2002

[67] Eddie Gibbs & Ian Coffey, *Church Next: Quantum Changes in Christian Ministry,* 2001, p. 129.

1. (Logic) Characterizing that kind of reasoning which deduces consequences from definitions formed, or principles assumed, or which infers effects from causes previously known; deductive or deductively. The reverse of a posteriori.

3. (Philos.) Applied to knowledge and conceptions assumed, or presupposed, as prior to experience, in order to make experience rational or possible.

Definitons from Webster's Revised Unabridged Dictionary

CHAPTER 11 - THE CONNECTING PIECES - 2: EXPERIENTIAL

holidays that I actually want to learn the books of the Bible in their chronological order for a sticker as a prize".

The starting point of anything we do with children needs to begin with their experience. Once again, Jesus modeled this in His ministry. He walked up to the woman at the well and spoke her language. He knew she was lonely, alienated, and desperate for love. For Jesus simply to talk to her would have been amazing enough. He knew that she was thirsty for so much more than water, and he started there. Even in his confrontation of the facts about her life, there was something loving and accepting and real about Him, so that instead of running away, she went straight to other people who had rejected her and told them they must meet this man too. The disciples were busy telling Jesus that he shouldn't be talking to a woman like that, but His concern was to help her at her greatest need.

With so many choices and options, Hugh Mackay considers that this generation (our children) feel mostly alienation, even within the clutter and choices this world has to offer them.[68] Are we addressing those issues?

The starting point of anything we do with children needs to begin with their experience

In an effort to teach the children about loneliness, I wrote a program called 'Lost in Space'. In the first lesson, I start by addressing the issue: "We all know what it feels like to be lonely". That is their experience. That is where so many of them are at. They might not admit that or even be able to verbalize it, but they sure do identify with the character 'Toggle' who is a space man – lost on a strange planet and very lonely. Throughout the program the children help him find Jesus and, ultimately, his way back home.

By Week 6 we address 'Jesus knows loneliness', but not before we have gone on a journey dealing with some of their experiences about the options we face when we feel lonely... It's obvious that we all have

---
[68] Hugh Mackay *Reinventing Australia,* Harper Collins, 1993.

choices about what we do when we want to quit. The great thing about Jesus is that He knows exactly how we feel. In the garden of Gethsemane, He sweated drops of blood in His anguish about what was before Him, and every time He went to his friends for support and help, they were asleep. He knows loneliness.

We are teaching truth every week, but we are starting from their experience. It is not good enough to teach something because we happen to like the story.

There are many other opportunities for experiential learning. We can allow them to experience Jesus' presence during worship. I remember a 10-year-old girl called Karen at one of our camps. She came from a non-Christian home and had no experience of Jesus and church until she came to *Kids Klub,* which I was running at the time. After a time of worship in song, I asked any of the kids who wanted to to come up and share anything that had made an impact of them that morning while they were singing. There was a long line of kids and she was at the end. When I got to her, I put the microphone to her mouth and she said something I will never forget. She said, "When we were singing that last song, I felt like Jesus was holding my hand." Most of the leaders, me included, were in tears. It was a beautiful moment.

Now I know she had not given her heart to the Lord, so should I have dismissed that comment, told her that she couldn't have felt that because she didn't officially 'know' Jesus? Of course not! God was working within her. He was just beginning, and it was through a worship experience that God was talking to her. She can walk away from my words that Jesus loves her, but it is harder to walk away from an experience of Jesus holding her hand.

It doesn't even matter if the experience doesn't go exactly as you planned. In one of my RE classes, I was reminded that the experience, no matter what it is, can be powerful. A small group of cynical, yet fun 10-year-old boys added spice to this class, and in this particular lesson, I was teaching the kids about the people who wrote the Bible and why they wrote it. I asked them, based on what we had been learning, what they might write in a book about God and Jesus. Dale (one of my cynical, yet sweet enough kids) promptly said, "I would write a story about David and Goliath and how the boy was able to kill the giant with one small rock". I was quickly thinking through this year's lessons and could not remember teaching that. So I asked him, "Where did you learn that? He said, "Remember last year when I was Goliath and you put me on that chair and then when Kaeman (who was playing the part of David) shot a marshmallow at me I fell off the chair and everyone laughed?"

As he said this, I remembered that it was about 18 months ago, and I remember thinking at the time, "Well, that didn't work..." All the kids were too busy laughing at Dale falling off the chair and I was too worried about him hurting himself.

Which comes first, the 'believing' or the 'experiencing'? I would say the experiencing. Dale remembered the whole story. I bet he wouldn't have if I hadn't tried to get them into an experience where they were part of the story even in the smallest of ways. We need to be continually thinking about the WAY we teach, as well as the content. You can put them into endless situations where they must experience something that might be a key to them coming closer to God.

A number of years ago, in my preparations for my teaching, I began to ask myself the question, "If I want to teach this to the children, how I can get them experiencing it?"

This was when I began to write programs for our own kids. Even today I will sit at my computer with a relevant issue that I want to teach the children. I will choose a relevant character out of the Bible who went through a similar experience. I will read the passage and ask God the question, "How can I get the children experiencing this?" Then the ideas flow!

We are here to build a platform so that kids can experience who Jesus is. It is not about

> *It is not about how well we teach; it is about how well we provide a platform for them to experience God*

how well we teach; it is about how well we provide a platform for them to experience God. I would like to think that you would not be reading this book, or working with kids, if you had not had a personal experience with God. I mean, why would you be doing this unless Jesus is real to you? If your answer is, "I haven't had a personal experience of God", then I suggest you put this book down and get to a quiet place with God and stay there until you do.

I suppose there are many reasons why we work with kids, and this book is not intended to deal with all those issues. I am sure that you can think back to a time in your life when God has guided you, spoken to you softly, challenged you and changed you. We all need these experiences and so do our children. The Bible never said, "Unless you become an adult you cannot experience the things of God". The Bible actually says the reverse. Yet so many ministers and adults teach in a way that reflects the belief that unless you are an adult you cannot understand the things of God.

So, how do we teach experientially?

I remember I was teaching the children the Ten Commandments and helping them see they are very relevant to today. When I got to the commandment "Thou shall not steal", I knew we were dealing with one of those topics in which you can get the 'right answers' from kids even though it is not how they really feel. Stealing is very common around the age of 8– 12 years. It is the time they start to pinch things for the thrill of it all! They are not going to admit to that. So, naturally, they are going to agree with anything I say.

I asked myself, "How I can get them experiencing this?" You're thinking, "What? Are you crazy? Are you serious?"... Yes I am!

I put partitions around the room to make a smaller space enclosed within the room that I was teaching in. I put a leader in there tied up and a couple of big men beside her with dark sunglasses on. When the children came in I informed them that 'Sally' was missing. Everyone loves a drama, so you can build it up as much as you like. I said to the kids, "But if we do exactly what I say, I think we can save her!

CHAPTER 11 - THE CONNECTING PIECES - 2: EXPERIENTIAL

We have to circle these partitions 7 times singing our favorite worship song. If we all do that 7 times, we can bust down those walls and save Sally, but we have to take only her and get out of there as quickly as we can.....Can we do it? Yeah...Let's go!"

We began singing our favourite songs. When we got to the 7th time, they burst through the walls in order to save Sally. The children suddenly saw lollies all over the floor and all over Sally. Naturally, all the kids suddenly lost interest in saving Sally and were in a scramble for lollies. As soon as this happened, I informed the leaders with dark sunglasses to come alive, chase the kids, take all the lollies and Sally and get out of there. Once I'd calmed the hysteria resulting from the experience, (remember it's an experience! Chaos is part of it!), I had a perfect opportunity to talk about stealing. In 10 minutes, I had put the children into an experience where they had taken something that wasn't theirs. We could talk about what happened, we could talk about the consequences, and I could tell them that if we had taken just Sally, we would now have Sally and all the lollies to share.

I then began to tell the children my own story – the time when I was 10 years old and was nearly caught shoplifting with my girlfriend in a Woolworth's store. We were going to take a chocolate bar each and get out of there. I got out, but my friend didn't. It was terrifying having the police take her, and although I wasn't caught, I learnt a very scary lesson. Stealing has consequences. The kids love to hear your stories, but you have to convince them that they are true because they put you up on a pedestal and think you can do no wrong. It is also important that they see the times you make mistakes so they can see that you are real too. The most important challenge, though, is putting them in an experience that they won't forget and that might help them make the lesson part of their own experience.

Experiential learning can be taught by starting with the kids' current experiences, as with the issue of stealing. It can also come through teaching in a way that causes them to experience during the process. 'Family Service Projects' are effective ways for the family to be experientially involved in something together. "The more that all the threads of the children's growth experiences are tied together, the stronger the imprint that will be left on their heart."[69] It should be a standard expectation in your children's ministry that every child be personally active in some form of ministry. The ultimate experience of Christ is when we begin to serve him. It is in this experience that God can truly transform us and change us forever.

THE ULTIMATE EXPERIENCE

> **The more that all the threads of the children's growth experiences are tied together, the stronger the imprint that will be left on their heart**

I was speaking to a pastor one day about a dream I have to take every child aged 11– 13 years on a mission trip. I feel strongly that our children today need to experience that Jesus is real. We are so blessed in this lucky country (Australia) to have so much, and to be able to freely love and serve Christ. I believe we could change a generation if every child that graduated from primary school went on a mission trip before they went in to high school.

These are the years that they are drawing conclusions about things that they might believe in for the rest of their life. This is the time when they should be putting their worldview to the test, stretching their faith and resources and doing something daring for God. They need to see the impossible happen and see that they can do something significant for someone else in the name of the Lord.

I was selling this idea to the pastor. He listened to my passionate reasons and my exciting dreams for the kids. He waited until I was quite finished and said, "Well, it would have to be something local". I was stunned and asked him why. His response was that it would cost too much money, it would be too dangerous for the children and he didn't think they could handle it. I said, "But the point is, it

---

[69] George Barna, *Transforming Children into Spiritual Champions*, Regal Books, Ventura, 2003, p. 113

CHAPTER 11 - THE CONNECTING PIECES - 2: EXPERIENTIAL

is supposed to be a stretching experience, it is supposed to be hard work – to raise the money, to be in a place that is not comfortable and to find ourselves relying on God!"

More saddening still was the fact that I was hearing again that all-too-common belief that children can't handle these things, that they don't have anything to offer until they become adults. By the time they have become adults we have a hard job on our hands trying to convince them that the Jesus of their Sunday school childhood faith (that didn't work then) suddenly will work now! We like to make hard work for ourselves. Instead of working with children when they are all fired up and want to learn and live for Jesus, we would rather wait until the light goes out completely and then spend our resources trying to light a new fire.

By taking them onto the mission field and letting the kids see the poverty, getting them involved in helping to build a house, they might believe and listen to what Jesus has to say about their everyday life. In a world where kids are experiencing so many things that are not of God and making choices as to whether they continue experiencing these things, we need to give them an experience of God. This is just one way that I believe children could have a life-changing experience.

I was personally challenged with this issue regarding my own child. My husband and I run a camp for abused children every year called 'Southern Cross Kids Camp'. This year, we took 43 children from the local area where we live away for a week of wonderful memories. Many of these kids are quite violent, very hard to connect with, and have great difficulty functioning in a social setting in what we would define as a 'normal way'. As a result, my children do not come to camp, and spend the week with friends and family. We explain to the children what we are doing, and they understand these kids often don't have a mum or dad or family and this is a wonderful thing we can do for them.

This year, however, I went to see my own kids midweek because I had to transport them from one place they were staying to another. My son Sam became very distressed and wanted to come to camp with me. My son was 9 years old at the time and he is a very sensitive, caring kid; goodbyes are always hard for him.

I was feeling torn, as I never want what I do in ministry to be a stumbling block for my children, and they share in ministry with us so often he didn't quite understand why he couldn't come to camp. In the end, he was so upset I said he could come with me and stay at camp, under very strict rules, and the understanding that he must always stay by my side and do what I say in case a situation arose where he might be in danger. This sounds dramatic, but with these kids, leaders come away with bite marks and bruises etc... regularly. I was fearing for him and wasn't keen for him to see these children's behavior, and yes, doubting that he could cope with it.

As I drove back to camp, I got a call from the other director saying that a little boy, Jordan (who I might add had spent much of the camp up to this stage in the fetal position) was finally going home the next morning. I haven't the time to explain why, but Jordan wanted to go home, claiming he hated camp and had no friends there. When I got to camp, I saw him and his buddy sitting quietly in the kitchen, not getting involved in what the rest of the camp was doing. I said to Sam, "See that boy there? He is lonely and doesn't have a friend. Would you like to go and play a game with him?" Sam said, "Sure, I would love to".

They played all night together, I saw Jordan smile for the first time. Jordan came and had breakfast with Sam the next morning. He came up to me after breakfast and said, "You know I am going home today." I said, "Yes, that is your choice". He asked, "Is Sam staying for the rest of camp?" When I said he was, Jordan asked, "Well, can I stay too?"

Sam stayed with him for the rest of camp. Jordan came out of the fetal position in the group time, and joined in, and at the end of camp was asking if he could come back again. Sam's gentleness and compassion made a difference in another child. Leaders came to me and said at the end of the week, "Your son already has your compassionate heart for people". I saw a beautiful thing played out: Sam ministering to abused children by using the soft, sensitive nature that God has given him. You don't have to go to another country for our children to be able to reach out to the hurting and the lost, but you do have to empower them and give them opportunities.

I finish with this story because I want us to all think about the many possibilities we could be using to empower our kids. Often the only thing that prevents these experiences is those in leadership positions who do not believe in children and the way that Christ sees them. I challenge you to not be someone who stops the children from experiencing Him.

Jesus says, "It would be better for him to be thrown into the sea with a millstone tied around his neck than for him to cause one of these little ones to sin" (Luke 17:2 NIV). A scary thought to finish with. Let's not be guilty of this.

> **You don't have to go to another country for our children to be able to reach out to the hurting and the lost, but you do have to empower them and give them opportunities**

 **A TIME TO REFLECT...**

1. Think of an experience in your life that had a profound effect on you. What happened, and what difference did it make for you?

   _____
   _____
   _____
   _____
   _____

2. Take some time out to think about the times that you have had an experience with God or a time when God has taught you something you will never forget. Take some time to write them down. You never know when you can share your experiences with the kids you minister to.

   _____
   _____
   _____
   _____
   _____

3. Take some time to talk to the kids you minister to and ask them about the times that they thought were the best experiences/ memories for them while under your ministry.

   _____
   _____
   _____
   _____
   _____
   _____

CHAPTER 11 - THE CONNECTING PIECES - 2: EXPERIENTIAL

4. Think about 2 new ways that you can empower the kids in your ministry to have a significant learning experience.

   _____
   _____
   _____
   _____
   _____
   _____
   _____
   _____

5. Discuss with your team the ways in which we need to be careful not to limit our kids' experience with God.

   _____
   _____
   _____
   _____
   _____
   _____
   _____
   _____

… PIECE BY PIECE - TAMMY PRESTON

The connecting pieces
3: 'EDUTAINING'
We need to both educate and entertain to communicate effectively

The world is full of entertainment. If we try to entertain our kids we will never do it as well as Hollywood or the XBox. Even if we try to simulate either of these, we will have missed the BIG picture of what ministry is about.

Likewise, our kids' world today is stacked full with education. They go to school 5 days a week. This is certainly how Sunday school began, but it emerged out of a need within the community at the time to educate people. We no longer have that need, as the formal education system does this on a weekly basis for our kids.

We need to do a mixture of entertaining and educating, not one or the other on their own. We want to teach children about Jesus and His truth, and we want this to be fun and engaging. We do not have the structure of the school system which requires children to be there. They will listen and learn if they choose to, and if they see it as valuable in their lives. This is where the 'entertaining' bit comes in – truth that is expressed in a way that is interesting. "Entertain, don't amuse. Do not be afraid to add to education the component of 'entertain' – hence the monstrous word 'edutainment'."[70]

> **Entertain, don't amuse. Do not be afraid to add to education the component of 'entertain' – hence the monstrous word 'edutainment**

I am embarrassed to say that even the local school is doing it better. I was a part of an Easter Service at my son's school one Easter. They had asked me to sing a few songs. I arrived early to set up and found that there was a special school assembly on to farewell a teacher. I decided to stay and be a part of it and was moved to tears many times as the children wrote and performed a 'rap' about the teacher. Then a dance group danced to his favourite song. It was great to watch, and the teachers did a great job with the kids in preparing them for this presentation. Then the children went back to their classes to return later for the Easter Assembly.

I was setting up when in walked three lovely older ladies carrying their little tape recorders. They set up for their items. I sat through a boring assembly where the Scripture teachers were oblivious to the fact that they were being made fun of by the children rather than being listened to. I couldn't help but be embarrassed at the comparison. I thought, "It is no wonder teachers in the school system don't take us seriously. No wonder children are bored". I was more moved that morning by a farewell to a teacher than the presentation of what Jesus did for me on the cross at Easter, and I love Jesus with all of my heart. When it comes to plain entertaining, we just don't do it very well, let alone actually teach something in a way that connects to our kids.

I see so many ministries start with some games and competitions, and then once the kids have had a fun time they are settled down

---
[70] Leonard Sweet, *SoulTsumani: Sink or Swim in New Millennium Culture,* Zondervan, Grand Rapids, 1999, p. 213

CHAPTER 12 - THE CONNECTING PIECES - 3: 'EDUTAINING'

for some teaching. Then you hear the classic, "Now, I have a leader watching at the side for the best girl and the best boy who will win a prize at the end of this time. So sit up straight and let's see who the best listener is." We have all been guilty of that over the years. We entertain and then we educate. I believe that we can do both at the same time.

There are number of reasons why this is so important to do:

- It needs to be fun and entertaining for the kids to take interest.
- We have so little time with these kids. Let's not waste a moment with pure entertainment. Let's make every moment count.
- The message is too important not to use the most powerful methods of teaching.

We must always remember the 'edu' part of 'edutaining', which is the *content*. Most ministries want their kids to understand the core values of the church and they repeat that each year, over and over again. This repetitiveness loses its freshness with children. The children feel they are not learning anything new. More effective churches, however, delve deeper with new insights and personal applications. They will look at a wide range of the stories of the Bible and continue to look at them from different angles.

There has been a tendency to go into highly technical productions with full technical video presentations to try to compete with Disney. Well, I can assure you, you might be good at that, but Disney will always do it better. We will also miss the real strength of what we can bring to the kids that no one else is doing.

I know that educators want to be able to quantify how much kids are learning. They like the teaching to be expressed in ways that can be measured. We all want to be able to measure growth, but that is not always possible. The best measurement I have found is to watch an 8-year-old begin developing in their gifts and abilities and then to start serving. By the age of 12, they are beginning to lead. This means that they have had to learn something, work through what it means to them, and have had the experience of seeing it work. They then continue to grow and become one of the key leaders. That all takes time, but it is a clear measurement that God is doing something in this person's life. We will be known by our love and by the fruit we bear.(See John 15)

The fact is that many of the kids you will minister to don't even want to be there. If it is not entertaining they will not engage. The other fact is that while they may not want to be there, they sure want to hear about how God can help them in their daily struggles. They want to be moved and challenged about something that is real.

> **We have got to stop telling nice stories and start edutaining them with the truth**

The message of Christ is moving and we should not be afraid to show it. The children we work with are used to seeing movies they should never be able to watch, which means they are seeing visuals which are very graphic. The kids we minister to are emotionally moved by TV and the heroes they idolize. They want to be like them. If you don't present a Gospel which shows a real Jesus, who sacrificed an incredible amount for them, you are not speaking on their level. We have got to stop telling nice stories and start *edutaining* them with the truth!

CONNECTING WITH EDUTAINMENT
Edutainment makes the 'point' *during* the process, not at the end.

Let's imagine you wanted to teach children about not giving up when the going gets tough. I believe we live in a "fast food" world, that has resulted in an expectation from kids that everything needs to be quick and easy. As a result, children are ready to give up too easily. I mean, giving up on playing a sport is one thing; giving up on life at such a young age is another thing entirely. So an example of addressing this issue might look like this: Putting the kids into teams and saying, "I have a challenge for you that is impossible!" You'll find most kids love to disprove that anything is impossible!

CHAPTER 12 - THE CONNECTING PIECES - 3: 'EDUTAINING'

The room we met in for one program was a gym hall and the ceiling was rather high. Before the kids came in I put helium balloons up on the roof. Then when the kids were ready I outlined the challenge for them. The challenge was to stay in their groups – consisting of seven kids and one leader – and get one of the balloons down from the ceiling. They weren't allowed to use anything else but their team. I gave them twenty minutes to see if they could do it. I put some music on and let them go for it.

Well, there were kids trying to scale the walls, while other kids were taking their jumpers off to throw at the ceiling. There were kids who gave up after five minutes and sat around the edges watching everyone else, while others started jumping onto each others shoulders in order to be able to reach higher. Watching all this, it was obvious that they were having a great time; but you could also see the kids who saw the hopelessness in it right away and quickly checked out of the exercise, happy to be spectators. I was watching and collecting data to really bring my point home about not giving up even when things are impossible. I wanted to teach them that it is all about giving it your best shot.

I was about to round it up when something started to happen in the middle of the room. Teams began to work together and they started building a human pyramid. They got to the second and third level, and then I started to worry about our 'Duty of Care'. I had leaders around the edges ready to catch the kids who might fall as this pyramid grew taller and taller. Soon the whole room was in on this. They finally got to the fifth level and one small child scampered up the kids' backs, and reached and grabbed a balloon! Well, the cheer went up, the kids' pyramid crumbled in laughter and celebrations, and the chant was on at me: "You said we couldn't do it!"

What an edutaining experience! Before they started, I had talked about the persistent widow and how she never gave up. But during this activity, they experienced completing what I truly thought was an impossible task; to say nothing of their experience of teamwork and valuing people's strengths (small ones for the top and strong ones for the bottom). The lessons went on and on. They didn't have to have it all explained. They were educated in an entertaining way and they were IN the learning experience. There's nothing better in ministry than when a teachable moment just flows. Are you setting up these edutaining options for your kids?

> *They were educated in an entertaining way and they were IN the learning experience*

EDUTAINMENT PLAYS GAMES WHILE TEACHING

Here is a way of teaching about being a hero for God. Our kids all have heroes and they are eager to be like them. We want to teach the children that God wants us to be His hero to those around us. To achieve this, we use the game show idea of 'Pick a Face'. We have posters of all their favorite heroes pinned up just as they are on the set of a game show, and when they answer a question, they get to pick the face of one of their favourite heroes. They answer a question about a hero in teams, and then pick a face for points for their team.

On one of the posters is a picture of an Australian child wrapped in an Australian flag. Her name is Kelly Fisher. She is often picked last because no one knows who she is, so she gets the most points and the team that picks her naturally wins. The cry always goes up, "Who is Kelly Fisher?" In the excitement of the game the kids are usually thinking, "She must be important, she has the most points", which lends itself to a powerful opportunity to explain that Kelly Fisher is an Australian child who loves God and that makes her a hero in the eyes of God. Jesus said that unless you become like a little child, you cannot enter into his kingdom... In the midst of a game, you have been edutaining.

EDUTAINMENT *ALLOWS* KIDS TO TALK AND DO THINGS

Let's begin with the basic concept of sin. I want to teach kids that we cannot get to God on our own merit because of the sin in our life. Believe it or not, we can have a simple but edutaining message

CHAPTER 12 - THE CONNECTING PIECES - 3: 'EDUTAINING'

about sin. You could simply get a plastic sheet and some dog food, or canned spaghetti, or anything yucky and dirty to spill onto the plastic sheet. Have a sign saying 'God' at the end.

Talk to the kids about who would like to be with God and why. Once most have decided that it is something they would like to learn more about, continue on. Get them to take their shoes and socks off. If you have a large group, ask three people to do so.

Challenge the kids that if they want to get to God they have to walk across this plastic, which might seem easy, but they need to know a few things first:

1. God is pure and perfect and cannot be with anyone who is dirty or imperfect.
2. Since Adam and Eve chose to sin, we have been imperfect and sinful.

Then you take some dirt and throw it on the plastic. Say to the children, "When we hit others, say hurtful things to others or hurt others, we sin." Get some spaghetti and throw it on the plastic. "When we decide that we are more important than anyone else and decide to live to please ourselves, we sin." Get some custard and throw it on the plastic. "When we decide to break the rules at school or at home or we break the law because we think we know better or we just want to be naughty, we sin." Pour dog food on the plastic. You might like to ask them what they did this week with their siblings, their school work, their playground behaviour, etc... React to what they say by pouring more stuff onto the plastic. Make sure there is enough dirty stuff on the plastic to ensure that anyone who tries to walk across has no chance of doing it without getting dirty feet.

Now get the children to walk across the plastic to get to God. As the kids do (and let's face it, it's is always fun to have dog food squirm though your toes!) they realize that they cannot be dirty if they want to get to God. Make sure they cannot get to the end without getting dirty. The point is we try, and yet we cannot get to God on our own. Even if we try to be the best we can, and even if there is only the smallest amount of sin in our lives, we cannot get to God. In fact, no one can be good enough to get to God because of sin in our lives.

The point is made, and more importantly it is remembered. The inevitable to be asked is, "How can we be friends with God then?" This can lead in to pointing them to the fact that we can only have a relationship with God because of what Jesus has done.

EDUTAINMENT HAS A LOT OF MOVEMENT AND ACTION (MOSAIC)

I remember one night when we presented the Gospel message to a group of children centred on the trial of Jesus. We had three stories going at the once (this is mosaic learning). With simple lighting and 4 actors as soldiers and the crowd, we re-enacted the whole thing.

I began as a judge, complete with gavel and big coat. The soldier and crowd would interject, and a huge cross was in the middle representing Jesus. Then I would change from being a judge to being me on the other side of the stage talking about a boy at a new school and how he responded to being falsely accused. We went from story to story, leaving the kids at pivotal points of the story each time.

The use of simple lighting can be very effective here. The solders and the crowd were fierce and angry, and the children could feel it. They identifi ed with the kid at school and how he might have felt. They watched how Jesus stood silent, never fighting back, always humble and gentle. While challenging the kids about self-control we had also re-enacted the trial of Jesus, so that by the end it was obvious how unfair it was for Jesus to go to the cross.

They felt it, and all the time they were being edutained. There was plenty of depth in the information that the kids were able to pick up if they wanted to. It was a moving message, and the children were able to debrief within a small group afterwards. We had over 80 kids give their hearts to the Lord that week as a part of the edutaining process. They saw something in Jesus that challenged them to want to give their hearts to the Lord and follow Him.

EDUTAINMENT WORKS BEST IN A *TEAM*, WHERE DIFFERENT *DYNAMICS* PLAY A KEY ROLE

As the previous example shows, there is much more that can be taught when you are working in a team.

One night I was teaching about the importance of every person; that they all have a place in the work of God, they just need to be prepared to use their gift for Him. The edutainment went something like this:

Leader Speaks:
(Italics is what action you need to do while speaking)
Now I am on a mission today. I have never been very good at cooking, it's not my strength. But we do have to eat, so it's something that I have had to work hard at. Tonight I thought I would make something for you all as a special treat – just something I want to share with you, because someone else shared it with me and it was really yummy. When you experience something good you want to share it. So, I thought I would make it for you...

Now, I have a set of instructions here *(you can display them on a screen or just read them out of a book)* and it lists what I need. Now, what I am really good at is getting the utensils all ready, so I've got a bowl, a spoon, a really nice apron – it's important to keep yourself clean and looking good – a plate to put them on, and a beautiful basket especially lined – I did that this afternoon – I wanted it to be just right for tonight!. All right, so I have got all the utensils ready – it took me all afternoon – but I wanted it to be just right!

Now, what's next – I'll just read the instructions. I need *(read out all the ingredients)* – Hmmmm....oops.....It seems that I have forgotten a few things. Oh ... this basket looks so good and I so wanted everything to be right for our time together. I can't believe I haven't thought it all through. I meant the best, but maybe we will just have to settle for the fact that I have tasted it and it is really nice. Let's just imagine eating one! I'll take this basket around and you can pretend – Hmm... Very nice... *(Try to get the kids to pretend to eat; notice and comment when they aren't doing it – for example, "Hey, what's wrong? Can't you pretend? What's your problem? Kids usually have good imaginations!")*

Look, I'm sorry; I tried to do my best. I told you that I was really good at the utensils bit! Don't you at least think I did alright there? I mean, I can't think of everything! I don't think that this was a good idea! Maybe I have bitten off more than I can chew!

(Looking dejected) (Begin to read out the ingredients again and, one by one, have leaders that have each been given one of the ingredients previously come up to add their little bit. You go along with it and get more and more excited as you get all the ingredients...)

Right now I need to... *(read instructions and have set leaders come and help you with set tasks like separating eggs, whisking, putting them on the right tray and putting them into the oven. Have the last leader organized to take the final product to the pretend oven and cook it for you.)*

Wow, I did it! I knew I could do it!

(Feeling proud of yourself) (React to audience as they prompt you to say that you did it with some help.)

(Then have a leader come in with a full tray of pre-made goodies ready to go, and if you have more kids then one slice tray, hide the rest somewhere up the front so you can make it look like they are multiplying! Next, put them into the basket and place them 'just so' – because your presentation is everything. As you are doing that, talk to them: This is your teachable moment.)

Wow – These smell so nice! I am so excited! You know, I could never have done this without the help of the other leaders. I just sat back and let others do what they do and now I get to do what I do well! See, my mission was to give something to you tonight that was really yummy! I would have failed if not for others doing their bit. This was a huge mission feeding all of you – *but* not as big as it would have been for the disciples when they were

CHAPTER 12 - THE CONNECTING PIECES - 3: 'EDUTAINING'

out with Jesus and he was talking to 5,000 people and he asked them to feed them! You thought I was starting to stress when I couldn't deliver my treat to you – imagine having to feed 5,000 people in the middle of nowhere!

Well, when Phillip was asked, he started working out how much it would cost and said, "Are you joking, Jesus? It would cost 6 months of my wages to pay for all that food!" Meanwhile, Andrew was talking to people in the crowd and noticed a little boy with his lunch. Imagine if that were you! Just about to tuck into your lunch and a man comes up and asks, "Would you be willing to share your lunch with 5,000 people?" Would you say, "Are you joking? I've just got some little sardines and some bread! It will be lucky to fill my tummy! Have you tasted barley bread? It's disgusting – Mum can't afford nice bread like the stuff at Baker's Delight!" Well, he might have thought that, but he said, "Sure I'll share! It's not much – but I'll let Jesus have it!"

See, Andrew just found something little and was willing to ask, and the boy was simply willing to give what he had to Jesus. THEN Jesus used it to feed 5000 people. That's our part in the mission! Will you take up your place in the mission?"

From there we moved into a time of prayer and ministry!

Do not underestimate drama, characters, simulations, pantomimes or story telling which all require a response from the children. They are all very powerful in the teaching process and can have a greater impact than the spoken word. Sometimes the most powerful teaching does not require words. Marcel Marceau spent his whole career communicating without words. Some of the most moving experiences I have had have taken place in complete silence. You can't always take a written test to show that you have been changed on the inside or moved from the heart. But edutainment has that power.

 **ACTION STEP**

1. Take some time to watch a popular show for kids today and study how they use drama, plot, and entertainment to teach a particular topic/issue.

The connecting pieces
4: RELATIONSHIP
Our ability to build relationships is the key to connecting to people today

No matter who we are or what we have or do not have, we all crave relationships. We need people who care about us, people who will listen and love us no matter what we do. As a result of all the technologies that are developing and of the many options from which our children can choose to spend their time today, relationships are in decline.

Leonard Sweet speaks of discipleship in terms of it needing to be 'incarnational' and 'relational'. When he speaks of being incarnational, he is talking about 'being there'. Leonard says, "The greatest compliment anyone can receive is 'Thanks for being there'. And the greatest condemnation anyone can make against you? 'You were never there'."[71] He talks about being real and not wearing masks around the people we minister to.

> **Leonard Sweet: The greatest compliment anyone can receive is 'Thanks for being there'. And the greatest condemnation anyone can make against you? 'You were never there'**

---

[71] Leonard Sweet, *Jesus Drives Me Crazy!*, Zondervan, Grand Rapids, 2003, p.36

Being there is also very much about understanding, living in and connecting with the culture that we are ministering to.

I have taught SRE with a particular class for three years now. They are now in Grade 5 – that tough age where they know everything and in just half an hour a Scripture teacher is somehow expected to come into the class and teach them all about Jesus. (It still blows me away that I can walk into the public school system and share the Gospel message every week if I want to!)

When I walked in for the first lesson this year, the kids let out a big cheer. The teacher was shocked and said to me, "I never get that response! Lucky you!" This has come out of relationship; it stems from both the way I teach and the time I have spent with these kids for over two years now. If I had to go into that classroom for the first time this year, they would probably be eating me for recess! But every lesson is a joy, and it is a thrill to build upon the message of Christ week after week through my relationship with them.

There was one lesson that I was supposed to teach on 'The authority of Christ'. I wondered how I could make this come alive to them. I walked in acting really stern and serious and scolded them when they spoke to me. I felt bad as I was doing it. I had just had my hair coloured and the girls immediately noticed and made a nice comment, but I quickly scolded them for speaking when not spoken to. None of them knew how to react, but they sat up and were very quiet and well-behaved as I continued the charade.

After five minutes, I couldn't take it any longer. (Mind you, they were so well behaved, I wondered if I should stay like this. But should my time with them be entirely about me having complete control or me being in relationship with them?) I said, "I can't do this any more! What is going through your heads right now about the last five minutes?" Relaxing now, they said they thought I had had a really bad day, or that I was losing it or something. This set the scene to talk about different types of authority. I wanted to focus on Jesus' authority and how it had its basis in relationship.

CHAPTER 13 - THE CONNECTING PIECES - 4: RELATIONSHIP

I placed a box in front of them: "If I told you that there was something special in the box that uniquely described everyone in this room, hands up who would believe me?" Everyone put their hand up. I then asked why they believed me. They said things like, "We've known you so long and always known you to be someone who tells the truth." While that was all very encouraging, it proved a point. Out of relationship – because of the authority I had as someone they trusted and respected – they all believed something that would otherwise be hard to believe. Out of relationship, I can teach this class of twenty kids who are not really interested in Jesus and what he can do for them, and have them totally there with me each week.

What a privilege! That is why I minister to children, because I have seen the impact we can have and I am passionate about the message. I am teaching them some important stuff, but it is the way we teach it that can make all the difference. With these kids, I could be the worst story teller in the world and it wouldn't make any difference. In the end, it is the fact that I have turned up week in and week out for over two years and share my life and the things I am passionate about with them that leads them to listen.

> *In the end, it is the fact that I have turned up week in and week out for over two years and share my life and the things I am passionate about with them that leads them to listen*

The radio commentator Paul Harvey has a saying: "Too many Christians are no longer fishers of men but keepers of the aquarium".[72] He believes that the Church needs to become less of an institution and more of a community.

I believe that effective ministry to children needs to be far more relational and far less institutional. Sunday school is one of the classic institutions of the Church. I believe it needs to be broken down and

---
[72] Leonard Sweet, *Jesus Drives Me Crazy!*, Zondervan, Grand Rapids, 2003, p. 97

rearranged. I challenge you to continue pressing forward and pushing the boundaries that are set within our Church structures. If people call you crazy along the way, then be happy to be a fool for the cause of Christ. You are in good company (2 Corinthians 12:11).

> *In the three years of his official ministry he spent the majority of his time with 12 people*

It seems too simple to say we need to spend more time with our kids. Yet anyone in a marriage or friendship knows that the breakdown happens when the time you have together begins to drop off. The latest trends in ministry to children have taken us into the video, DVD and computer world, and those resources can be very effective. But if they begin to replace relationships with real people and the importance of spending time together, then we are missing one of the most powerful examples of Jesus when he came to this earth. In the three years of his official ministry he spent the majority of his time with 12 people.

It is important to note that Jesus' involvement with these men wasn't simply based on signing up 12 disciples to 3 years of Bible College and key conferences and then allowing them to begin ministry when they graduated. This was classic on-the-job training. It sometimes meant sink or swim (literally for Peter) and 'doing' life together. There is value in formal training, but not in isolation. I think that sometimes formal training has actually encouraged the view that children cannot minister until they are older. The bottom line is, everything hinges on *personal time* and how we choose to spend that *personal time.*

In the western world, nearly all children have a TV in their house. Many have a TV in their room. Most have access to a computer and the latest games on either the Internet or on their own personal Game Boy or Xbox. But many of them never have a real person they feel they can talk to. In the work I have done with children in 'Divorce Recovery' programs, I have been surprised how few children feel that they have an adult they are comfortable talking to about anything.

CHAPTER 13 - THE CONNECTING PIECES - 4: RELATIONSHIP

While visiting the US in 1997, I was taken to a store called the 'Incredible Universe'. It was a huge warehouse where you could buy every electrical item for the house that you could possibly imagine. They had a child minding facility at the entrance. You exchanged your child for a beeper so you could be contacted at any time should anything happen to your child. So what? That's not unusual these days, even in Australia. But as we walked in to drop off our friends' children, I was stunned by what I saw.

Having worked with kids for many years, I knew that any place with 30 or more children in it must be noisy, a hive of activity and hard work for the minders. We walked into a silent room and as I looked around I saw children glued to monitors, TV screens, computers and electronic games. There wasn't even much expression as they played the games. (They obviously haven't played the ones I have!)

The children we were with quickly found a spare monitor and the trance began without so much as a goodbye. I was amazed and dumbstruck. I couldn't get that picture out of my mind. I went home and wrote the 'Actual Reality' teaching program mentioned in Chapter 10 after that experience.

I based the dramas around a couple of kids who live next door to each other and catch the bus home each day from school together, yet never actually talk to each other. They go home and get onto their computer and play this game of basketball over the Internet. On the computer they are champions. They didn't know it, but they were even playing each other. The picture is sad as they face each other on their computers, literally with walls between them, and yet they are never friends. One day there is a power surge and the street is blacked out. They are bored and have nothing to do and discover that they live next door to each other and that they had been playing the same game on the computer. They begin to play ACTUAL basketball and in that experience are challenged with conflict resolution, team work, communication, but mostly the value of REAL friendship. Our world today is not teaching them these skills because they are not skills that you can learn on the Internet.

If this is in fact the world they spend most of their time in, my question is why – in the limited time you have with these kids on Sunday morning or a Thursday afternoon – would you put them in front of a TV o or computer again?

> *The idea of incarnational presences corresponds to the idea of locality. Jesus moved into the neighborhood; he experienced its life, its rhythms, and its people from the inside and not as an outsider*

So it is with the 'institutional' church. We need to be 'incarnational' in ministry to truly understand ministering through relationships. "The idea of incarnational presences corresponds to the idea of locality. Jesus moved into the neighborhood; he experienced its life, its rhythms, and its people from the inside and not as an outsider".[73]

Frost and Hirsch speak of mission in relation to what Jesus was talking about when He said, "I will teach you to be fishers of men."(Matthew 4:19NIV) Today when most of us think of fishing, we think of one person, one rod and a lot of time. The fisherman must know the tides, know where the fish are and be patient in the hope of finally catching a fish. In the time of Jesus, Frost and Hirsch believe the statement would have painted a very different picture for the disciples; a picture which they believe is more aligned with the incarnational model they are talking about.

The disciples were fishermen by trade. They fished with a net. It was all about dragging a large net across the bottom of the sea. If the nets were strong enough and had no holes they could catch anything that was in their way. So, in order for the disciples to catch fish, it wasn't a matter of patiently sitting in a boat and waiting for the fish to bite; rather, much of the time was spent fixing and mending their

---

[73] Michael Frost & Alan Hirsch, *The Shaping of Things to Come: Innovation and Mission for the 21st Century Church,* Strand Publishing, Erina, 2003, p. 39

nets on the shore. This meant that when they did go out fishing they would catch more fish with their good quality nets. Frost and Hirsch suggest that "the web of relationships, friendships and acquaintances that Christians normally have makes up the net into which the not-yet Christians can swim. We believe that the Missional-Incarnational Church will spend more time on building friendships than it will on developing religious programs."

I have worked with foster children who have nothing and with kids in the most opulent areas of Australia who are rich and have everything that whistles and bangs. Yet both desire the same thing. At the camp we run for abused children where children experience a week of wonderful created memories, an adult leader is assigned as a buddy for one to two children. That buddy's job is to spend all week with these kids. They listen, they play, they walk, and they experience so many things together. These children are starving for someone to spend time with them.

I have also run a *Kids Klub* in Sydney's Sutherland Shire. It is considered one of the most affluent areas in Australia. They couldn't believe that we (adults) would actually choose to spend each Thursday afternoon with them without being paid! Many of them were at *Kids Klub* because their alternative would have been to be home alone or at some other childcare facility after school finished until their parents got home. But we were not child-minding. We were having fun, playing, building relationships and teaching them about the one who wants to have a friendship with them more than anything in this world.

"The spiritual search of Generation X does not consist primarily of an intellectual quest. This is not a generation seeking answers to the philosophical questions that have preoccupied Christian apologists such as arguments for the existence of God, the origin of the universe, the believability of miracles or even the deity of Christ. They are not interested in listening to people who presume to have all of the answers. Rather, they want to meet people who have a transforming relationship with God."[74]

> **They are not interested in listening to people who presume to have all of the answers. Rather, they want to meet people who have a transforming relationship with God**

This connecting piece is a vital part of what we are about. The time you spend relating with your children will reflect how important it is to you in your ministry. Over half the time we spent in 'J-Zone' – the Sunday Morning ministry with children – was in relationship-building activities. That is how important it is to what we do week in and week out in ministry to our kids. This means that much of the curriculum we might be using doesn't get used! (Shock! Horror!) This might mean you need to de-program!

This is something that many children's workers struggle with. The new curricula that are coming out are strongly DVD and video driven. It is a struggle to keep the balance. I have a whole team of people who work with our kids and are called 'carers'. Their sole purpose is to come and love and care and play with a small group of children. They say to me often, "I don't really do much here ...not like you do". I always respond by telling them that they do the most important job of all. Relationship is the foundation upon which anything lasting and valuable is built.

We have kids who can't wait to get to J-Zone – not because they can't wait to see what Tammy is going to teach them today, but because they can't wait to see their small group leader, or they can't wait to see what happens in the drama. The drama is another way for kids to identify and build relationships with the characters they come to know and love. They journey with them as they discover what Jesus will teach them today.

---

[74] Eddie Gibbs & Ian Coffey, *Church Next: Quantum Changes in Christian Ministry*, 2001, p. 129

CHAPTER 13 - THE CONNECTING PIECES - 4: RELATIONSHIP

I have involved many different kinds of people in children's ministry who would never have considered working with kids because they couldn't possibly sing or do a craft with them. But they can play and listen and talk to them about Jesus in one on one discussion. They say, "I can do that". We need more of these people and we need more time for what they do. The mentoring concept – where adults come to be a grandma, a grandpa, an uncle or an aunty to children – is so important. The kids may have relatives or they may not...We can never have enough.

If our ministries are so full of craft, videos, music and teaching that we don't have time to know the names of the kids, which sport they play or their favorite hobby, how can we truly know them? This is the platform upon which we begin to activate our kids towards Christ. This issue is so vital that I say to my leaders, "You can be the worst story teller in the world, but the kids will hang onto every word you say if they know that you love them." If your kids love you, they will listen to anything you say. So much of our learning comes out of relationship, and we need time for those relationships to build.

Even our teaching (in the traditionally formal sense) needs to be relational. I watch many good communicators with kids and often wish I had their ability to hold their audience and capture the kids' attention. But I have learnt over the years that this might be fine for a visiting speaker or a one-off ministry experience, but it just doesn't cut it with the kids long term.

I have changed the way I communicate to kids a great deal over the years. I have started to be more 'real' with them and share stories of my life and struggles. At first it was scary because I would be embarrassed or feel vulnerable. At times I have even cried. I remember having just finished a camp where I did most of the speaking, although we had brought in a guest speaker for one of the night sessions. She was funny and entertaining; kids loved it and they loved her. They talked about the fish she waved around for the rest of the camp. But when the evaluations came in, the feedback indicated that what had impacted the kids the most were my sessions and the ministry times we had in J-Zone (our worship times). I was curious to know why that was.

As I talked with one of my colleagues about it, he suggested something interesting. He said, "As good as the other speaker was, she didn't have any stories". I have already said I don't see myself as a great speaker or worship leader, but when you minister out of relationship, when you tell your stories and share your life with the kids, you have an impact. I have come to believe that this is the critical difference.

> **Life-changing ministry is not so much about great and wonderful presentations as it is about relationships**

It gives us all hope that we can have a powerful impact on kid's lives. Life-changing ministry is not so much about great and wonderful presentations as it is about relationships. It requires being 'real' with these kids first and foremost, and being willing to 'go with the flow' no matter where that leads.

Please don't misunderstand me. We need the evangelists and the great communicators to come in and slam us; but the ongoing ministry and growth comes as we live week in and week out with these kids, through the ups and the downs, the good times and the bad. That is where the connection to the 'real' issues comes.

Jesus modelled this in His own ministry. He had three years to change the world, to speak a new message. How did he choose to use this time? If it were me I would have been out traveling the world, speaking at as many Temple Conferences as I could, aiming to speak to as many people as I could in a limited amount of time. What did Jesus do? He spent most of His *time* with 12 people, building a relationship with them – changing their lives 'from the inside out'. Then they went out and impacted a few more and then a few more. That is how Jesus chose to do it because developing relationships is the means by which He believed He could have the most profound effect in someone's life.

CHAPTER 13 - THE CONNECTING PIECES - 4: RELATIONSHIP

As a teacher, this goes against my training. I learnt at Teacher's College that to teach effectively there must be a thin wall between you and the students. There was a line that we knew we mustn't cross. If we crossed it and became their friend, we risked losing the power of authority, the ability to discipline; we feared that they would see this as weakness.

I know many ministers today who still have a guard up. They believe that in order to be an effective minister you must be strong, always in control and never let anyone see the real you. Sunday school came out of a model based on the schooling system in England. As a result, we think teachers need to always be in control, always know everything and maintain distance between ourselves and the ones that we teach. Well, I don't see Jesus behave that way. His disciples saw him when He was eating, sleeping, tired, angry and even sad. Because they lived together they saw him on all occasions. Jesus made time for people and so should we. It must be our priority. It is the key to connecting with our children today.

A TIME TO REFLECT...

1. What relationships do you treasure? Why?

2. What is it about these relationships that are special?

3. Do you mentor someone younger than yourself? If not, spend some time with God asking Him who you need to be investing in?

4. What children are you investing TIME in on a regular basis? How are you doing that other than teaching them the word of God in a formal structure?

5. What stories do you share with your kids? Are they personal? Do they know the real YOU? Do you know the real THEM?

6. What free time is there in the programs you run for just "hanging out" together?

_____
_____
_____
_____

7. Have you ever taken the time out to watch the kids you minister to play sport, do a concert or get an award?

_____
_____
_____
_____
_____

8. When you are aiming to teach something – ask your self how you can relate to the kids in a personal way – so that they might be able to be a part of the experience and journey it for themselves personally.

_____
_____
_____
_____

9. How much of your ministry is running programs and how much of it is being with kids in real life situations?
   For example: Sleepovers, playing sport, going to the beach, BBQ's, camping trips, hanging out doing fun activities, tutoring etc...

_____
_____
_____
_____

PIECE BY PIECE - TAMMY PRESTON

What keeps a puzzle together?

Love, communication, understanding our differences and encouragement can be considered the 'glue' of ministry – elements of design that keep the puzzle fitting perfectly together

Have you ever thought about what keeps a puzzle together or how a puzzle seems to stick together without any glue involved? It's like there is this invisible force that locks it all in place. We know, actually, that it is the way the pieces are cut to form curves and slots that helps the pieces interlock together. Have you ever thought about why the pieces of a puzzle have curves and slots? Why they are not just all square pieces or made of similar shapes?

The answer is obvious, but only when you think about it. A bunch of squares can sit beside each other and play their part, but one bump and they are separated. There is nothing that allows for movement and helps them stay together. In fact the big picture will never be clear for very long if we have nothing that intertwines us and keeps us together. You can have brilliant people and ideas, even great facilities and resources, but if you have nothing that connects you or keeps you together it will eventually fall apart.

The glue that brings a team together is not rocket science. We are all familiar with it. However, I believe that actually 'living it' is the hardest part of being in a team that works towards bringing children to Christ. Let's face it, we are all people, and sometimes I wonder why

God devised a plan that relies on humans to actually get the message of Christ out to the world, because that requires that humans work together. On top of that they have to work mainly in a voluntary capacity. That combination in the natural world is a recipe for disaster, and yet when it works in the supernatural there is nothing like it!

I have worked in wonderful teams and also in teams that have been soul destroying. The difference has had more to do with this 'invisible force' rather than the lack of resources, people or ideas. What exactly are the curves and slots of a puzzle that keeps us together?

LOVE

> *There must be a love for what we are doing, who we are serving and a love for one another*

1 Corinthians 12 says you are just a "clanging bell if you have no love". Love is that four-letter word that is so wonderful and yet so difficult at the same time. In ministry it needs to be the glue that brings us all together. There must be a love for what we are doing, who we are serving and a love for one another.

This is not a requirement for a normal work situation in the world. We can love what we do, but we don't have to love the company or the people who work in the company. Sure it helps, but is it not required when you take the job. We can even love the company and the people but not love what we do. We can love the job and the people but not the company and still work in the job. In ministry, though, we need to love all three if we are ever going to be effective. Of course, there is love and there is 'love', and that difference needs to be defined. When you look at how God calls us to love, it is very challenging. It is a huge job description.

COMMUNICATION

Communication is harder than we think. Communication relies on the people you are communicating with actually getting what you are saying. Simply 'saying' something does not always mean that you have communicated it.

CHAPTER 14 - WHAT KEEPS A PUZZLE TOGETHER?

I have led many teams where I have felt that the process has been spelled out very clearly but then someone inevitably says, "I have no idea what I am supposed to be doing". If you know anything about learning styles (or if you are married), you would know that this is because we all learn and listen differently. We need to appreciate that what will make sense to one person will be 'gobbledygook' to someone else.

A good team will be made up of different types of people, which makes it more important to be communicating in many and varied ways, and as often as we can, to help everyone remain on the same page. A well-functioning team will mean people having very specific roles to play and understanding that if they don't play their part in the team something will fail to happen. This needs to be clear to everyone.

Whether you lead a large team, a small team or a team within a team, or you are a team member, your communication can make or break what is happening and ultimately the big picture can become distorted with 'in-house' issues that people can't get through. Communication is a key in any relationship. It is sometimes something we need to work harder on than anything else.

> **Communication is a key in any relationship. It is sometimes something we need to work harder on than anything else.**

COMMUNICATION CAN BE A BONDING EXPERIENCE
Nothing bonds people together more quickly than a tragedy. It is often during the saddest experiences of all that we best understand the need for pure love and togetherness.

I have been a part of a ministry which ministers to abused children for six years now. In Australia, the ministry is known as 'Southern Cross Kids Camps'. It was begun in the USA (where is known as 'Royal Family Camps') by Wayne and Diane Tecsch in 1985.

The aim is to give these children who have been abused in one way or another at least one week of happy memories.

This team comes together each year for training about 4 months before the camp, and after that we work together for a week. This is an intense, exhausting and testing time in so many ways, and yet there is an incredible connection which pulls all of us together to face some of the saddest/happiest times of ministry that I have ever had.

The team is a large one, allowing a ratio of 1 adult to only 1– 2 children. Our jobs are all well defined and we spend the 3 training meetings presenting the puzzle to the team and very clearly outlining what their parts within it will be. By the time we get to camp everyone is on the same page.

Communication is a real key in this ministry. Everyone must understand their role and expectations. By the time the campers come and everything begins, we need to know exactly what we are doing. The only surprises then will be the ones that the kids bring – and there are many of them. We are prepared for most of those surprises, too – at least in general terms.

These children need a lot of love and attention, and if we don't understand that this is the purpose of our being there, the whole thing will fall apart. Everything is planned. Everything is discussed beforehand to ensure the program has no 'holes'. There is never any time when the children are alone, and the leaders are trained in every aspect of the day and how they are to respond to whatever eventuates. In fact, they are actually overloaded with information before camp and often walk in scared and prepared for the worst. But this is the best way for them to be ready for anything.

A connection begins at the beginning of the training period as we all see the intensity of the ministry and the incredible value of the things we can bring to a child's life. We set up pathways of communication for all kinds of issues. We ask that all leaders have someone praying for them during camp, and that their own communication with God is refreshed and renewed before they come to camp. We have a psychologist available for them throughout the week to talk about anything that is going on. We have a support system of aunties and uncles and grandmas and grandpas and pastors available to talk to throughout the week and support them; and all this is just for the leaders!

We communicate openly and honestly about what is going on every morning of camp and bring it to God through prayer as a group. We have a debriefing time at the end of camp which is very intense but so important before they go home. Communication is very hard work and extremely necessary, but it is amazing the way it cements together a diverse group of people in such a short time.

THE WAY WE COMMUNICATE HAS CONSEQUENCES

I have also been on teams where we could be in a team meeting and suddenly find out that a whole system had changed without any prior knowledge and everyone had to just fit right into it. This kind of team situation fosters doubt, fear, lack of trust and disunity. This kind of communication does not allow people to own the new system, or be able to feel confident that they even have a place in the way things will function. The more the team can be a part of the process of change and new directions, the more that people will be able to move with the changes. The way we bring about change can strengthen a team or weaken it.

> **Shady communication and see-through promises never pay a dividend – only division**

"Shady communication and see-through promises never pay a dividend – only division."[75] A team I worked with in a local church had within it a group of people who I called my 'Key Leaders'. They were people who had key roles in different areas of the ministry, which meant that

---
[75] George, Hunter, Kennon, Callahan, Toler, *The Pastor's Guide to Growing a Christ like Church,* Beacon Hill Press, 2004,p. 45

every ministry area within the children's ministry was represented. They were also people with leadership abilities, enthusiasm and ideas. I would meet with them 5 times a year to discuss change, strategy, ideas and possibilities.

I would communicate to them my dreams, new ideas and possible future directions and they would be a sounding board. They were invited to be a part of the process, to dream with me, to add their ideas, or at least to say how they felt about the new ideas. It was important that everyone felt heard and was able to communicate their thoughts on the matter. During this time the ideas would grow, change, be added to and more importantly, owned. I loved the ideas that people came up with, and they often brought so much more to the original concepts.

Brainstorming and 'think tank' sessions like these are great communication activities for a team to be a part of. By the end of those meetings, 8 – 10 people would walk away excited about the new things that we were going to do as a team. I had my key leaders tell me that those 'think tank' breakfasts were some of the most exciting meetings that they attended all year.

This kind of communication is so important for helping people in a team move forward together. The consequences are that people feel like they are part of the process, they own it, they talk about to their own teams and they are willing to be a part of the process to see it happen.

If you are the leader in a situation like this, you need to be confident enough to hear feedback, consider other ways of doing things and allow people to give alternatives. You also need to know when things are heading in a different direction and be able to reign them back in, or else to be open to new directions which might have the same result but achieve it in a slightly different way.

COMMUNICATION IS ESSENTIAL FOR HEALTHY MINISTRIES

It is important to always remember that in children's ministry you are working within a larger team. You may be working within structures that have many teams. It is easy to get so involved in your own ministry that you forget that you are part of a larger team. For some reason there has always been a gap between children's ministry and youth ministry. I think this happens because we are all too often egocentric, and naturally we think that OUR ministry is the most important. We should not feel like we are competing with each other for resources or volunteers.

I have made some big mistakes in this area because of my zealousness for building teams and expanding children's ministry. As a result, I have stepped on toes in other ministry areas of the church, like the youth ministry, the women's ministry or the singles ministry. Good communication between all the ministries in a church can avoid this.

Often we are isolated by the times we work; we pass each other in the halls but don't really talk to each other about what's happening in each others' area of ministry. I get so 'purpose-driven' that I have to look up and see what others are doing sometimes and take the time to listen. This might involve something as simple as planning an event on the same day as another key ministry area.

Ensuring this doesn't happen requires good communication. The volunteer drive is a big one. I have been in meetings and watched team leaders fighting over new people in the church in order to have them in their ministry. I remember sitting quietly watching this happen and thinking to myself, "It sounds like a competition!" Then suddenly someone said "Well, Tammy steals all the good ones anyway!" I was taken aback by this and realized that if people felt that way about me, we needed to talk about it. I was under the impression that when people wanted to serve, they came and volunteered their services and we accepted them and trained them. This began a whole conversation where I was asked to talk about how I recruit people, as a few team members admitted that they were struggling.

When people are insecure or struggling in their areas of ministry, communication can become more like complaining and arguing instead of sharing and encouraging. A healthy team needs to work together, not against each other. When you are in a larger church, even dates on a calendar and room allocation can become a topic for debate. Good communication can change these issues from being a problem to being opportunities that encourage us to value each other's ministries.

> *Good communication can change these issues from being a problem to being opportunities that encourage us to value each other's ministries*

This is also important amongst the various churches in your community and beyond. There is nothing worse than 'competing systems' in this area. I have run key events in the area, only to find that another church down the road is running a similar event on the same day. I ask why we couldn't do this together. It is very sad thing when you ask that question and discover they are often not interested in working together. There is so much to be gained by 'joining forces'.

The encouraging thing that I have found in interdenominational situations is that children's workers in Australia have generally led the way with working well together. We are good at sharing events, teaming together and communicating about key events. Just recently I had a call from a church down the road which was conducting a survey of all the ministries and key events that churches in the area were planning for next year. This was to make sure that when they made their own plans they didn't to do anything that others were doing, but instead found the holes and tried to fill them. They said that they would rather connect the community into what we were doing well, and look at other ways to connect with the community themselves. To me, that seems like worthwhile communication!

CHAPTER 14 - WHAT KEEPS A PUZZLE TOGETHER?

UNDERSTANDING OUR DIFFERENCES

It is not a natural thing to want to spend time with someone who is very different from us. We often spend our lives avoiding those people while surrounding ourselves with people who are much like us. While this is fine to do in certain area of our lives, ministry is not one of them. If we truly understand the 1 Corinthians 12 passages, which speak about the body, we know that the Church – and hence ministry – will include all types of people.

While I love relating to like-minded people, you need people with skills that are different to yours to be able to minister effectively. Because of this they will probably also be different to you in many other ways. Whereas in a job situation you might find that certain occupations attract like-minded people with like-minded learning styles and similar behaviour, this is not always so in the church. The church is like one big extended family and as they say, "You can choose your friends but you can't choose your relatives."

The glue that will keep a diverse group together will be the unity that you have in Christ, the joint purpose you have in serving children, and the acceptance and celebration of your differences. I have found it is one thing to accept that we are all different and another thing to celebrate that.

Within the morning programs at a church where I was ministering, we included drama, music, games, administration issues and morning tea, as well as ministry and teaching needs. Clearly, it takes a team of people to do all those things, and we know that people with administration skills are often very different to people with creative arts skills. It is important that these people have an attitude of working together or there will be tensions that get in the way of ministry to the children. You'll have the dynamic of someone who focuses on the detail (administration) alongside someone who is a 'big picture' person (creative). There needs to be good communication, relationship building, and most importantly, a respect for each others' strengths and weaknesses.

I deliberately try to find staff members who can cover my weaknesses. I know that if I don't do that there will be countless key things that won't get done.

The *Veggie-Patch* age group (ministering to children aged 3– 5 years) would never have glue, stickers, play dough or pencils if it were up to me. I would simply forget about those kinds of details. If it were left up to me, the children would never have morning tea... My own children are lucky to get fed at times when I am focused on something that I want to get done! Luckily, I have kids a little like me (or maybe they have learnt that's just the way it is in our family), because they never ask for food and also get carried away with what they are doing. Suddenly, Dad walks in the house and it is dinner time and there is nothing prepared!

I have to know myself and my weaknesses. I make sure that there are people in the team who will sort that out. This means that people whom I have grown to love and respect will ask me things, and while my first response might be, "Who cares?" I bite my lip instead, stop what I am doing (which I always feel is much more important than what they are asking me), and answer them. Administration people are imperative to any organization. They are 'details' people and they think of everything. It drives people like me crazy, but I would never be effective without them, and am so thankful for them!

How diverse is your team? Are there people who rub you the wrong way? These are good questions to ask. I often had my team leader at one church say to me, "Why is that person working with you? He/she would drive me nuts!" My reply would always be, "Because they are great at what they do, and that is the key." Leaders who struggle with working with anyone that is different to them limit ministry, because they find it hard to see things from another person's point of view.

Meetings can often be really frustrating with a group of different people. There have been times when I've wished I wasn't the leader of some meetings because you do need to be on your guard and strong at times with a group of diverse people. But that is what leadership is about in the Christian community. We are supposed to be listening to each other, and we need to work towards a win-win for the whole group. If we can't lead the way when it comes to respecting our differences, then we have no hope of making a difference within our communities for Jesus. It is certainly something that can help the puzzle stick together' or else pull it apart.

ENCOURAGEMENT

I am amazed how desperately the art of encouragement is needed today. Children and adults alike are craving encouragement. It doesn't matter how good you are at something, we all need encouragement. I remember talking to someone I considered one of the best children's speakers in Australia. I thanked him for what he had said in a session and talked about how it helped me. He nearly cried on the spot. I was taken aback by his response. He then shared that he couldn't remember the last time someone had encouraged him in that way. He talked about his hate mail, the rude letters that people had sent him, but couldn't remember when someone last said, "Thank you".

> *If we can't lead the way when it comes to respecting our differences, then we have no hope of making a difference within our communities for Jesus*

Now, he may have been going through a particularly difficult period at the time, but I was shocked that this was how he felt. How can this be? I thought about it and realized that maybe when people are as talented and gifted as this man was, we feel overwhelmed and embarrassed about saying something to them. I know that's how I feel sometimes. I think perhaps this is an Australian thing, since when I go to America there is definitely a different atmosphere. We Aussies need to be much more encouraging to people, regardless of what they do. You have no idea the difference it can make to a worker to simply say, "Thanks – you have done a great job!"

As the leader of a team, I see it as my responsibility to make an effort to acknowledge people, to thank them, and tell them as often as I can that they are valuable. I could spend my whole time doing this and it still wouldn't be enough. Your ministry is as good as your weakest team member. It's so sad to see the number of people who leave ministries discouraged. It just shouldn't be so high. People need to leave a volunteer position or ministry area being celebrated, no matter what they do. If you are the team leader and you find this is a hard thing to do, find someone you can bring onto your team that is good at it.

I admit that this is also a weakness of mine. I have to try hard to be encouraging to everyone as I get so caught up in what needs to be done that I forget to stop and say thanks. When we run our camp in September each year, I work with over 70 leaders for one week. I have a person on team who does nice things for them all week. It is important that your leaders feel cared for and encouraged. My big task at the end of the camp is to sit down and write a thank you note to every one who has been on team. I try to write something personal that I have appreciated about them.

I remember a number of years ago, when I was particularly focused on speaking and leading worship at the camp, that I found when I got to the end of the camp and sat down to write my thank you notes, there were a number of leaders that I did not even know well enough to say something personal. I was upset with myself, and from that year on I have made a big effort to talk to everyone at camp who leads, and take more time out to get to know them.

I know that as things get larger, however, this becomes impossible to do. This year, we discussed beginning a mentoring system where my key leaders mentor 6 leaders both before and during the camp. When the idea came up, I initially thought, "This is going to be a whole new structure to set up. It will take a lot of work, and it will take away my role of leading them and give it to others." But my key leaders said they wanted to release me to be able to lead the big picture and give me less to do.

I have to be honest with you. I was thinking, "Why? Aren't I doing a good job?" I was feeling discouraged, but tried to keep an open mind and hear them out. I then realized that this was the only way to truly encourage this growing team. To have a group of key leaders who wanted to take that on and make it happen was exciting. I could have continued to think, "They are taking away my leadership here"; but as I thought about it, I actually could see that it was releasing me from something I am not good at and allowing me more opportunities to serve with my unique gifts. At the same time, it would ensure that there was a continued spirit of encouragement. In fact, it would be even better than it had been the previous year. In the end, it doesn't matter who does it as long as it is done and people feel encouraged, supported, valued and loved.

THE GREATEST GIFT OF ENCOURAGEMENT IS TO BELIEVE IN THEM

I am amazed at the number of people who have never had someone that actually believed in them in their entire life. I have come to realize that one of the greatest gifts my parents have given me has been their undying belief in me and that I could do anything I put my mind to. It has been an empowering force in my life to know that whatever I chose to do, my parents were 100% behind me. Even when I wanted to go into full time ministry – and I know deep down it wasn't what my dad would have chosen for me to do in life – he was always there. Now he is one of my greatest encouragers, and I am so grateful for that.

If you want to cement your puzzle and your team in a powerful way, then let them know you believe in them and empower them in their gifts and callings. "Servant leaders multiply their leadership by empowering others to lead".[76] It means we have to be other-focused, giving them the power and authority and the glory. The best thing you

> **Servant leaders multiply their leadership by empowering others to lead**

---

[76] C Gene Wilkes and Calvin Miller, *Jesus on Leadership,* Tyndale House Publishers, Carol Stream, 1998, p. 27

can do in an intensive ministry like children's ministry is to empower others to do the ministry. It is the only way it is going to get done.

We must remember that our calling is to see people (adults and children alike) come to know Jesus and grow in all that He has in store for them. If we are not encouraging and empowering others to 'fly' for Jesus and seeing amazing changes in people, then we are not fulfilling our mandate. "Leaders who are unwilling to trust those they lead will never see them break out of low-skill patterns of dependency. Growth comes through being given something to achieve"[77]

When Jesus walked this earth he didn't spend his time (limited as it was to three years of ministry) saying, "Look at me! Look at me!" He spent his time building and teaching and empowering others to do the ministry. If you want the puzzle to stick together, there must be some key leaders you are empowering; even if that means that they might do a better job than you one day. You need to be encouraging enough to say, "Go for it! I will be the number one member of your cheer squad."

Mark 6:7 says that Jesus sent his disciples out and gave them all authority to minister to those they came across. Are you giving others the authority to minister or are you holding it all to yourself? I remember when there were three children in our ministry who wanted to be baptised. It is always a wonderful thing when someone wants to be baptized; even more exciting when they are so young and have the rest of their lives to serve Jesus. One of the children was very close to my intern at the time and I asked her if she'd like to baptise that child. It was such a thrill for her and for the child. It made sense to me that it was the right thing to do, and we all shared the experience together. Later that day, the intern's dad came and thanked me for giving his daughter the opportunity to be a part of the baptisms. It wasn't until then that I even thought about it. I could have just baptised all three children. I am the Children's Minister after all. But

---

[77] K Gerard,"*Getting a grip on the Future: Without losing a hold on the past*", Monarch, London, 1999, pg 249

that is not what it is all about. It is about empowering others, and giving them authority and the joy of ministry.

Allowing people to flourish and grow is such an encouraging thing to do. The greatest gift you can give to someone is simply to believe in them.... "Good Leaders grow people, bad leaders stunt them; good leaders serve their followers, bad leaders enslave them."[78]

> **Good Leaders grow people, bad leaders stunt them; good leaders serve their followers, bad leaders enslave them**

THE POWER OF THE WORD

Don't underestimate the power of a kind word. It really doesn't take much effort, but it can change lives. The power of a word can cause people to walk over 'hot coals' for you, or stab you in the back before you know it. Decide that your team ministry will have an atmosphere of positive talk, not negative talk. You, as the leader can change the whole atmosphere of the team and the work environment.

In this way we really need to lead by example. I have experienced the power of being around positive people and the drain of being around negative people. I have been responsible for inspiring people and disempowering them with my words. It is such a scary concept that there are times I just don't want to open my mouth!

I have had people repeat to me something that I said 10 years ago which hurt them, and I don't remember even saying it. I can remember words that have been spoken into my life from years ago that still haunt me. We all know stories of children and adults who are scared for years because of a single comment made by someone in their past.

The power of our words to build up or destroy is terrifying. As a speaker, the huge responsibility we have frightens me. We should be

---

[78] Sir Adrian Cadbury quoted by Des Dearlove Article,: *'First Learn To Be a Follower'*, The Times, London, 9 February,1999

frightened! We must never forget the power of words over the kids we minister to. If the feel of the leadership team is negative, it will have a ripple effect that goes right down to the children. We all know those people who we love to be around because when we leave their presence we feel inspired, encouraged, happy and uplifted. Oh, how I dream of being that kind of person! But I know that I am not. I am a questioner by nature. I always want to ask, "WHY?", and that can sometimes sound like I am being negative. I am aware that this is a problem of mine. I am also very serious most of the time, and I need to deliberately surround myself with people who are going to lift me up and knock me out of that serious zone.

CHAPTER 14 - WHAT KEEPS A PUZZLE TOGETHER?

TO THINK ABOUT

1. When has there been a time that you have experienced "Loving Communication"? How did it make you feel?

   _____
   _____
   _____
   _____

2. Think about a time when you have had positive experiences of Communication within a team, either when you were the leader or a part of the team. What were the elements that made it a positive experience for you?

   _____
   _____
   _____
   _____

PIECE BY PIECE - TAMMY PRESTON

Can the picture change?
Needs and ministry are always changing; some things never change

Having completed our puzzle, we begin to celebrate the pieces coming together and how exciting it looks. It is important to take time to celebrate the great things that are happening in your ministry, but it is also important to always be evaluating its effectiveness and continuing to grow.

If you find that something is not actually growing and being effective, does this mean you throw out the whole puzzle and look for another one? I believe there are some things that never change and others things that will always change. The framework with which the puzzle of effective ministry to children is put together will never change, but the content and tools you use can always be changing. The resources you utilise and the programs that you are running today may not work tomorrow. There is no problem with that. In fact, that is what makes it exciting and fresh for everyone. Evaluation is always the key to successful ongoing ministry.

SOME THINGS NEVER CHANGE

The guide picture will never change. God's plan since the beginning of time has been that everyone might be in relationship with Him. This will never change. Jesus will always want the children to come to Him, that He might love them and help them fulfill their destiny in Him.

The corner piece will never change. Jesus always needs to be our corner piece. In John 15:4-5 he says, "I am the vine. You are the branches. If a man remains in me and me in Him, he will bear much fruit: apart from me you can do nothing". The Scriptures make it very clear that anything we do in our own strength is useless. Jesus must be at the centre of everything we do and at the heart of every new direction we take.

> *Jesus must be at the centre of everything we do and at the heart of every new direction we take*

THE VITAL EDGES WILL NEVER CHANGE

You will always need good leadership, an understanding of the community you live in, a commitment to build strong and healthy teams and the desire to help children grow in God. This means you need to have a pathway that guides them through that process. How you achieve these things might change. As the needs of the community change, so you will need to reassess what leadership you need, how the team needs to change, and in what ways you can improve the process of discipleship to move with the changing needs of your children.

The glue that keeps it all together will also never change

You will always need love, good communication, an understanding of each other's differences, and encouragement. Of course, there will always be new and fresh ways to make sure that these remain the glue which keeps the puzzle together.

HOWEVER !!!!

NEEDS AND MINISTRY ARE ALWAYS CHANGING

So, what will change? I'm glad you asked. The present picture is always changing. Nowadays, this takes place almost daily. Keeping up with the latest for our kids is an endless occupation for some. Thank goodness there are those authors and investigators who do make it a full time job to keep up with what is needed to connect with our ever-changing society. It is our job to remain open, to keep reading and watching the world we live in to identify the changes that are significant for our kids.

In short, we need to be doing everything we can to be sure we don't share George Barna's experience, who wrote in his book with regard to the church and children's ministry, "In retrospect, my view was so far off the mark that I didn't just miss the boat – I missed the entire ocean!"[79]

THE KEY IS HOW WE VIEW CHANGE!
For our kids today, change is a part of life. Sometimes it seems that we change simply for change's sake, and I do struggle with that at times. Often we throw away perfectly good things just because there is something newer. New is not always better. But change is part of Western culture. It is the world our kids are immersed in and we need to understand that. Whether we like it or not, it exists!

It is so important to get beyond the view that says, "Well, in my day......", or "When I was a little girl...." We may long for those days, but I can see my 11-year-old roll his eyes when the sentence begins. Ultimately our kids are saying to us, "Get over it!" And we need to do that if we are going to be able to view change as something we need to go with.

I have had the privilege of speaking at many conferences over the past 15 years. During that time I have seen many changes and observed many ministries that just can't change. It has been interesting to watch the 'old school' and the 'new school' and the chasm that has formed between them. There is a fine line between accepting that we are all different and respecting that, and being able to accept that some things have changed forever and there is no going back.

HOW THINGS CAN CHANGE....
20 years ago I took over directing a camp for children aged 8– 12 years at Stanwell Tops, NSW, Australia. When I was 10 years old, I had

---
[79] George Barna, *Transforming Children into Spiritual Champions*, Regal Books, Ventura, 2003, p. 12

been at this same camp when one night after a worship time, while I was waiting for hot chocolate, I felt I heard God whisper in my ear. He wanted me to be baptised. 10 years later I was directing the camp. As a result, it is a ministry very close to my heart. I have been at Stanwell Tops for one week in September every year of my life since I was 8 years old. It won't surprise you that I have seen many changes in this time. What changes are permanent? Have all the changes been necessary? Is it better now than then, or just different?

These are good questions to ask when you are working through what needs to change.

WHAT CHANGES ARE PERMANENT?

When I was 8, the camp was called 'Mini Midgets'. When I began as the director, this was the first thing I felt we needed to change. Not only is it now politically incorrect to use that term, it is a name that kids will not relate to; but the final straw was when the campsite had a group of short stature people onsite at the same time. Imagine if they had walked in and the notice board declared, "This way to the Mini Midgets Camp"?

> *Can we go back? No*
> *Have the changes been necessary? Yes*
> *Is it better now than then, or just different? Different*

When I was a camper, we called everyone 'Aunties' and 'Uncles. This was the second thing I changed when I became the director. Kids in Australia don't tend to like using titles with people. It might be sad that there is not much respect for that kind of thing, but that is the way it is. I have had new leaders come to me over the past few years, look at me and say "Hi! You were my Auntie Tammy when I was at camp!" Not only does it make me feel old, it is a reminder of how much has changed.

> *Can we go back? No*
> *Have the changes been necessary? Yes*
> *Is it better now than then, or just different? Different*

CHAPTER 15 - CAN THE PICTURE CHANGE?

When I was at camp we had on overhead projector, a piano, and a clown doing funny tricks. Now we have a full sound system, a band, and a data projector with a full technical team and everything that bleeps and buzzes. We have a number of professionally trained teachers who have a gift in communication, and a very professional drama team.

> *Can we go back? No*
> *Have the changes been necessary? Yes*
> *Is it better now than then, or just different? Different*

When I was 8 we had a lovely old couple who cooked for us. Now the site fully caters for all camps because of strict laws regarding the standard and safety of food.

> *Can we go back? No*
> *Have the changes been necessary? Yes*
> *Is it better now than then, or just different? Different*

In fact, when I think about the camp, it has transformed in countless ways. It is probably on the way to more significant changes in the next 5 years. As a child who had a profound, life-changing experience there, it would have been easy to say, "Well this is how we used to do it! It worked then...This is how I got saved, so if it was good enough for me it will be good enough to kids today!" That would be crazy, but I hear similar comments so often.

In essence, however, so much of it hasn't changed at all:

- We still present the Gospel to over 200 kids every September
- We still have a leader in a cabin with 5 kids and that leader loves and cares for them and shares Jesus with them
- We still do outrageous activities and have a blast
- We still eat three meals a day in a big hall. It's still noisy every meal time
- We still teach the campers things that will change their lives, and pray that God will meet them at camp and challenge them

- We still see kids make life long friends at camp

... *all* just a little differently.

There are some things that will never change and some things that must always change. We need to view change as a vital part of moving forward and pray along with Reinhold Neibuhr:

> *GOD, grant me the serenity*
> *to accept the things*
> *I cannot change,*
> *Courage to change the*
> *things I can, and the*
> *wisdom to know the difference.*[80]

---

80 Reinhold Neibuhr, 1926

A FINAL REFLECTION

The evaluation process is always a helpful one. Take the time to think about these questions:

1. What are some things that need to change in your ministry?

   _____
   _____
   _____
   _____

2. Make a note of the things that will NEVER change and place the list somewhere you will see it as a reminder of what is important.

   _____
   _____
   _____
   _____
   _____
   _____

3. Take some time to reflect on the past 5–10 years of either your ministry or your life serving Christ
   - What has needed to change?
   - What has been painful to change?
   - Have the changes been necessary?
   - Is it better now than then, or just different?

   _____
   _____
   _____
   _____
   _____

CHAPTER 15 - CAN THE PICTURE CHANGE?

Engage

The Discovery Learning Series is a suite of teaching resources that covers the whole Bible in 4 years, creating active & engaging learning experiences for kids aged 8 to 12.

●Discovery Learning Series

Tested and refined over two decades, this material will equip your church to teach your kids effectively, with the aim of creating meaningful faith encounters that last a lifetime.

www.discoverylearningseries.com

Discover

Faithful, flexible, thoughtful & affordable, this series is focused strongly on the child and the most effective ways to teach them.

THE WHOLE BIBLE IN 4 YEARS

The full 4 year curriculum features Lesson Plans, Activities, Games, Songs, Dramas and Stories. Each of the 16 modules (around 10 weeks each) explore a theme, using key stories from different parts of the Bible. Completing all 16 will give children both a strong understanding of the entire Bible AND the overarching story of salvation through Jesus.

GET A FULL TERM - OR A SINGLE SONG

Work through the term modules, in any order, or pick and choose from our huge library of Curriculum resources. Search by Scripture reference, Bible Character or Themes.

The Discovery Learning Series has been developed and refined over 20 years, under the leadership of Tammy Tolman, an internationally respected leader in Children's Ministry. Over that time it has been used in Sunday Schools, Church camps and Kid's Church with tens of thousands of children and across a great number of churches and denominations.

●Discovery Learning Series www.discoverylearningseries.com

www.ingramcontent.com/pod-product-compliance
Lightning Source LLC
Chambersburg PA
CBHW071609080526
44588CB00010B/1075